A Lillenas Drama Resource

TWO FOR MISSIONS

Courageous Stories Come to Life Through Readers Theater

by David H. Robey

Featuring

FOR THIS CAUSE
The Ministry and Martyrdom of John and Betty Stam

and

BRIDGE OF BLOOD
Jim Elliot Takes Christ to the Aucas

Lillenas Publishing Co.
Kansas City, MO 64141

Copyright © 1988
Lillenas Publishing Company

All rights reserved. No part of these scripts may be reproduced by any method whatsoever. PERFORMANCE RIGHTS for these works are granted when 10 copies of this book are purchased.

BRIDGE OF BLOOD based on *Through Gates of Splendor,* copyright © 1957 by Elisabeth Elliot, and *Shadow of the Almighty,* copyright © 1958 by Elisabeth Elliot. By permission of Harper & Row, Publishers.

Contents

To the Reader.................................. 5
For This Cause................................. 7
Bridge of Blood............................... 29
Glossary...................................... 53

To the Reader . . .

These plays were written with the dramatic readers theater style of performance in mind. As this concept of staging may be unfamiliar, I have included stage directions in the script to provide some help for the reader and/or director. Some basic blocking and set diagrams, along with a glossary of terms, are also provided. (Director: An understanding of the glossary will greatly help you to visualize stage movement techniques. I would also like to suggest a book on readers theater: *RT: A Readers Theater Ministry,* by Todd V. Lewis, published by Lillenas Publishing Co., Kansas City.)

Two of the basic concepts of readers theater that will prove most interesting to the director are the use of scripts and the use of "focus." By the former, I mean that the cast may legitimately use scripts as they perform the play. If a totally memorized route is not followed, I would suggest the use of scripts for the entire narrator's part and for all the letter and diary entries. Even though the action in the short sketches is limited to pantomime and facial expression, the use of scripts may be an impediment. Therefore, if possible, memorized lines may prove to be superior to read lines in the short sketches.

The term *focus* refers to the visual placement of the scene. This will be clearer after a brief examination of the three types of "focus" the director has to use. They are: (1) onstage focus, (2) offstage focus, and (3) a combination of the two.

On stage focus means that the readers relate to each other on the stage, sensing each other's presence, sometimes even turning to the person being addressed and actually establishing eye contact. This is the traditional system of establishing contact onstage.

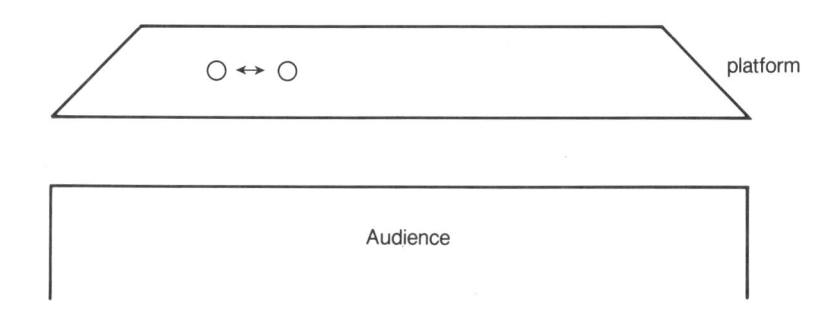

"*Off stage focus*, by contrast, refers to the technique of having the readers envision the scene out in the audience, of figuratively placing the scene of action in the midst of those witnessing the performance." The characters usually stand beside each other but do not actually look at each other. Facing the audience, the performers "see" the person being addressed or listened to, in their mind. If good concentration and intensity is exercised by the performers, the audience will find themselves drawn into, and actually participating in, the conversation.

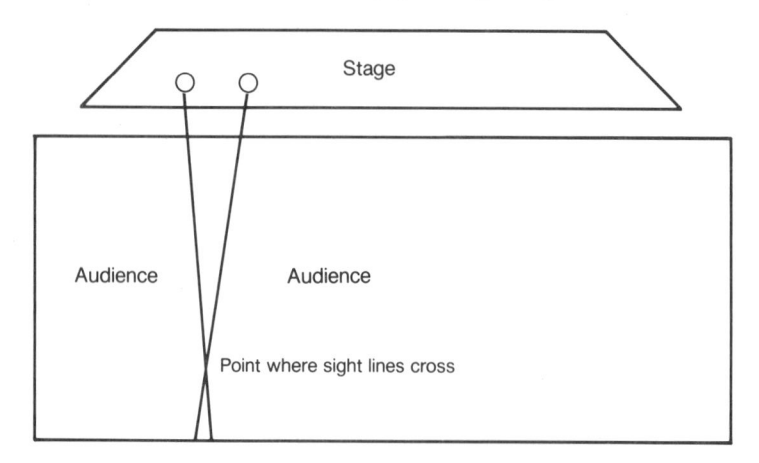

Notice the change of focus point with multiple characters.

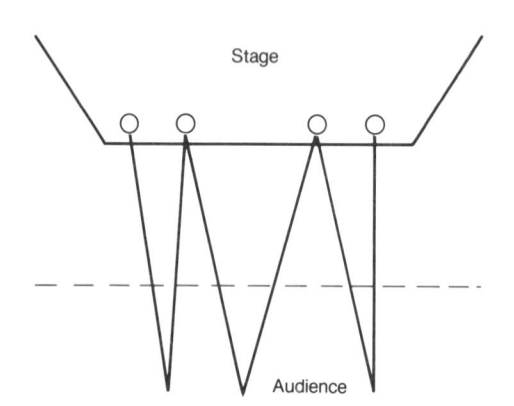

Moving heads slightly to new focus points gives the illusion of "seeing" new speakers.

By putting the focus point in the audience and causing the audience to envision the scene in their minds, performers are not dependent upon costumes or setting. Performers can wear conventional clothing and do a fine job of portraying the characters in the play.

I hope that these comments will be helpful to the reader and to the director. Directors, may I again suggest the obtaining of the fine book by Coger and White. I pray that God may bless you as you read these plays. "For This Cause" and "Bridge of Blood" are not fiction! All of the letter and diary entries are authentic. May those of us who know the Savior be inspired to serve Him more in light of the lives of these modern-day martyrs.

—David H. Robey

FOR THIS CAUSE

The Ministry and Martyrdom of John and Betty Stam

Cast:
CHARLES SCOTT (CH): *father of Betty Scott Stam*
CLARA SCOTT (CL): *mother of Betty Scott Stam*
JOHN STAM (J): *missionary*
BETTY SCOTT STAM (B): *missionary*
READER NO. 1 (R. 1): *male who portrays: opening reader, Kenny Scott, Mr. Page, soldier No. 1*
READER NO. 2 (R. 2): *female who portrays: opening reader, Helen Scott, Mrs. Page, servant girl*
READER NO. 3 (R. 3): *male who portrays: opening reader, Laddie Scott, Dr. Hiram, Rev. Torrey, soldier No. 2*

Props:
six metal stools
two swords

Sound Notes:
Organ music is used throughout the play, and a soloist is needed to sing "O Perfect Love."

Stage Arrangement:
Diagrams appear throughout the script indicating actor's positions. The following symbols are used:

        ○ —Stools
Initials —Actor's positions
        △ —Actor's back to audience
        ▽ —Actor facing audience
        ↑↓ —Actors move as per direction of arrow.
            Also indicates how stools are moved.

ACT ONE

(Stage arrangement of stools. Stools remain in this position throughout the performance unless otherwise indicated.)

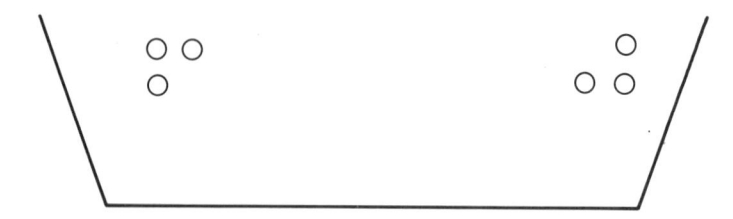

(Opening blocking of characters. Characters stand with heads bowed. They raise heads just prior to speaking. The three opening speeches are spoken directly to the audience in the form of radio bulletins.)

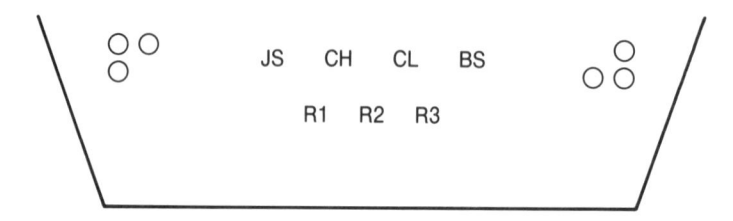

R1: A rumor has just reached the U.S. embassy in Shanghai that two American missionaries in central China have been kidnapped by Chinese Communists. No further details are presently available.

R3: Reports have now been confirmed that Mr. and Mrs. John Stam were captured in the city of Tsingteh. A ransom demand of $20,000 has been made to the China Inland Mission.

R2: The China Inland Mission has just made public information they received this morning. Yesterday, December 8, 1934, Chinese Communists executed two American missionaries, Mr. and Mrs. John Stam.

(READERS *move to side positions leaving* MR. AND MRS. SCOTT *in center stage. Consult stage directions.)*

(READERS 1, 2, and 3 *are seated with backs to audience and* JOHN *and* BETTY STAM *are seated facing audience with heads bowed.)*

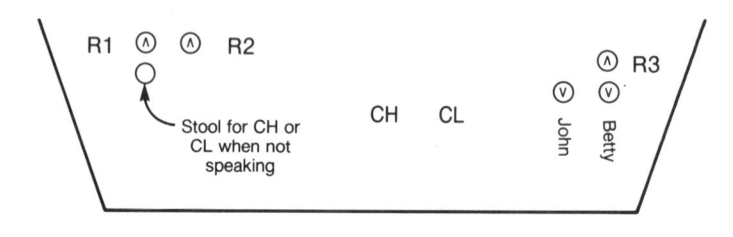

(CHARLES *raises head and takes a step forward, intense look of concern on his face.* CLARA *raises head and sees* CHARLES *in offstage focus. She knows his concern and tries to encourage him to return to his work.*)

CL: Charles! *(He does not hear her, so she speaks louder.)* Charles! *(He looks up and sees her in offstage focus.)* Have you finished the letter? *(He shakes his head "no.")* Dear, we promised the mission that we would have it ready for printing tomorrow.

CH: I was thinking of Betty. In my head I know that she is gone, but in my heart I just can't bring myself to believe that they killed her. Why would God allow that?

CL: Charles, you can't continue like this. Even though we may not understand why, it was in God's will. I know that you believe that!

CH: I want to believe that . . . but oh! . . . how I miss her. Why is it that we never love people enough when they are still with us?

CL: I found something yesterday . . . among some papers. *(She finds and opens a Bible in pantomime and takes out a paper.)* It's a poem. I don't know who wrote it, but it seems to say what is in my heart. *(She hands him poem in offstage focus. He begins to read slowly, but as truth of poem reaches him he reads more rapidly.)*

CH:
      E'en for the dead I will not bind
         My soul to grief—
      Death cannot long divide;
      For is it not as though the rose
      That climbed our garden wall
      Had blossomed on the other side?
         Death doth hide,
         But not divide!
      Thou art with Christ,
      And Christ with me
      In Him united still are we.

We still have her, Clara, our little daughter Betty. Even the great thief "death" could not steal one of God's children. I'll go work on the letter. Clara, forgive my weakness.

CL: Charles, a father's love for his daughter is never a weakness. (CHARLES *moves to stool *SR and drops out of scene.* CLARA *addresses the audience in conversational manner.*)

CL: The death of Betty was hard on all of us but especially on Charles. Mothers bear daughters, but fathers cherish them. They were so different and yet so alike. Charles, the great historian, scholar, spirited preacher, and Betty, like a deep-flowing stream. Yet they shared a great love: a love for life, a love for love, but supremely, a love for God, and a love to take the story of Christ to China.

*See Glossary for stage direction abbreviations.

(CLARA *moves to SR to stand beside* CHARLES *who still has his head bowed out of the scene.*)

> Betty first came to China in 1906. Born on February 22 of that year, we arrived in Shangtung Province, China, in October. My husband and I, along with little Betty, were eager to begin the work in China to which God had called us.

(CHARLES *comes alive, interrupting* CLARA, *and speaks to her in onstage focus. The goal of the interruption is to inject humor.*)

CH: Now, before that, tell them of the crossing. (CLARA *shows some reluctance at this suggestion.*) If you don't, I will.

CL: Well *(cautiously)*, I was nursing Betty, and Charles was worried that something awful might happen.

CH: There we were! Almost two solid months on the Pacific Ocean and nothing to feed our baby should something happen. Clara could have gotten sick or any number of things.

CL: Well, I didn't get sick and nothing happened. Except the boat sank.

CH: Oh, not the boat that we were on. But the boat sank that had all our clothes, furniture, medical supplies . . .

CL: wedding presents, books, my mother's china! Everything that we had brought from America.

CH: All was lost. I saw God's hand so clearly. Instead of our baby experiencing difficulty from being weaned from her mother, the mother and father experienced difficulty being weaned from the things of this world.

CL *(addressing* CHARLES *in onstage focus)*: Charles, you really must work on the letter. The mission thinks that our thoughts on John and Betty's death could be a great challenge to many people.

CH: I do so want to say it just right. Not full of self-pity and hate. Clara, God can use what has happened to our children.

CL: Yes, He can . . . and will.

(CHARLES *lowers head and* CLARA *crosses in front of* CHARLES *DSR.*)

CL: Life in China was so simple, it now seems. Our five children grew up in an atmosphere of love and faith. Love of family and faith in God. Along with a love for picnics, summers at the ocean shore, and ricksha rides through busy city streets, there was, of course, playtime with Daddy.

(READERS *1, 2, 3, and* BETTY *come alive and move from stools to indicated position while laughing and shouting as children. When they are in position,* FATHER *comes alive and moves DS.* JOHN *remains on his stool out of the scene, and* MOTHER *watches the scene with onstage focus.* FATHER *and* CHILDREN *use offstage focus.*)

CH *(raising his voice to be heard above the children's voices)*: Now . . . we shall continue with our baseball game. Let's see, whose turn is it to bat?

KEN Age 6 (R1): It's my turn!

LA Age 8 (R3): Oh no, Kenny! You're too little to bat!

KEN: I am not! I can hit the ball just as good as you.

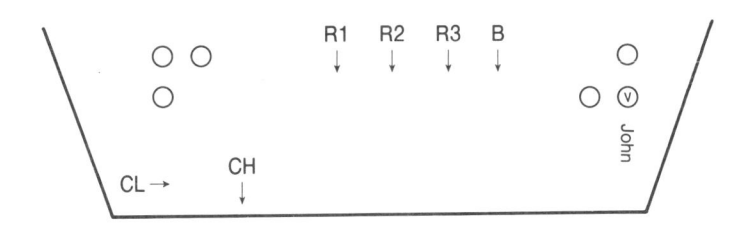

```
\                   R1  R2  R3  B                    /
 \    O O           ↓   ↓   ↓   ↓         O         /
  \   O                                  O Ⓥ       /
   \                                        John   /
    \       CL→    CH                              /
    _____↓_____/
```

LA: Father! Don't let him bat. I can hit the ball real good!

HEL Age 11 (R2): Laddie, you batted last yesterday. You can't bat all the time. We have to share.

(All children begin to beg and ask to bat, causing general chaos.)

CH: Wait just a moment! Helen, who is the umpire this week?

HEL: Betty is.

CH: All right, Betty. How will you settle this dispute?

B Age 14: Well, Laddie is right, Kenny is too small to be a very good batter. (KEN *frowns severely.*) But the umpire has decided to help him hold the bat so that between the two of us, we can hit that ball so hard that Laddie will never catch it. C'mon, let's play ball. *(Children all laugh and clap as they return to stools.)*

CL: Not every day had a playtime like that. Sundays were days for reverence and no foolishness. People today might think that we were too strict, but the children loved us for not only demanding righteousness from them but also living it in front of them.

In 1923, the family came to America on furlough as it was time for Betty to go to college. She had applied at Wilson College in Pennsylvania, but before entering college, the Lord had some teaching to do, so Betty went to bed with severe inflammatory rheumatism. Betty loved the out of doors, and this confinement to bed was most distressing. But it was in this bed of illness that she first began to realize her gift for writing poetry. Her heart never regained full physical strength, but the tenderness, sweetness, and sensitivity to God's voice that she learned during this time remained with her all her life.

Betty looked forward to college in a very special way. Thoughts of the future, perhaps marriage, were very prominent. However, Betty had decided that she would not waste time with arbitrary dating. She knew what kind of husband she wanted. In August 1925, prior to her first year in college, she wrote:

(BETTY *comes alive and moves to CS. She addresses audience as* CLARA *watches her.*)

B: I'll recognize my true love
     When once his face I see;
　For he will strong and healthy,
     And broad of shoulder be;
　His movements will be agile,
     And quick and full of grace;
　The eyes of Gallahad will smile
     In his so friendly face.

　He will not be a smoker,
     A drinker, nor a cheat;
　He'll know the art of tongue-control;
     He'll know how much to eat;
　His common sense is excellent,
     Basically sound;
　And cool in any crisis
     His judgment will be found.

　He will not be a rich man,
     He has no earthly hoard;
　His money, time, heart, mind, and soul
     Are given to the Lord.
　Oh, if he ever finds me,
     My answer, "Yes" will be!
　For I could trust and cherish
     Him, to eternity.

(BETTY *stays CS and lowers head.*)

CL: It was before her second year in college that Betty truly came to know a new life in Christ. After attending a summer Bible conference, she wrote a most wonderful letter.

B (*comes alive and addresses audience*): I have now surrendered myself to the Lord more than I have ever realized was possible. Already, He has wonderfully answered my prayers, in little things and in big ones. Among other things, I have dedicated to Him whatever I have of poetic or literary gift. Maybe He can use me along that line.

It has taken me some time to decide that I wanted to be a missionary, and the main reason against my finally deciding was this: the fact that I am a missionary's daughter and that everyone just naturally expects you to do the same thing, missionary work, myself. You understand what I mean, don't you?

I don't know what God has in store for me. I really am willing to be an old-maid missionary, or an old-maid anything else, all my life, if God wants me to. It's clear as daylight to me that the only worthwhile life is one of unconditional surrender to God's will, and of living in His way, trusting His love and guidance.

(BETTY *drops out of scene.*)

CL: After her death, we found a note that she had written in the back of her Bible, dated August 3, 1925. She called it her "Covenant with God."

B: Lord, I give up my own purposes and plans, all my own desires, hopes, and ambitions and accept Thy will for my life. I give myself, my life, my all, utterly to Thee, to be Thine forever. I hand over to Thy keeping all of my friendships, my love; all the people whom I love are to take second place in my heart. Fill me and seal me with Thy Holy Spirit. Work out Thy whole will in my life, at any cost, now and forever. "To me to live is Christ and to die is gain."

(BETTY *moves back to her stool as* CLARA *speaks to audience.*)

CL: Upon graduation from Wilson in 1928, Betty enrolled in Moody Bible Institute in Chicago, to train in the missionary program. It was during her second year at Moody that Betty met John Stam. John was a tall, handsome man and Betty . . .

CH (*interrupting* CLARA; *he stands, moves to C, and speaks to her in onstage focus*): Clara, I've almost finished the letter. Please go and read it and tell me if I've left anything out.

CL: I'm telling them about how Betty met John.

CH: Well, now, I can tell them about that.

(CLARA *moves to the stool* CHARLES *sat on and sits, bowing head.* CHARLES *speaks to audience.*)

CH: They met at the weekly prayer meeting in the home of a Mr. and Mrs. Page. The Pages were repesentatives of the China Inland Mission, and several students met in their home each Monday night for a time of prayer and fellowship. As Betty felt her leading to go to China, she attended faithfully. It was at the Page home that the courtship began.

(READERS *move into position: bring two stools to set stage for Page home scene. All* READERS *have heads down and* JOHN STAM *has his back to audience. Participants in scene use offstage focus while* CHARLES *and* CLARA *watch the scene on stage.*)

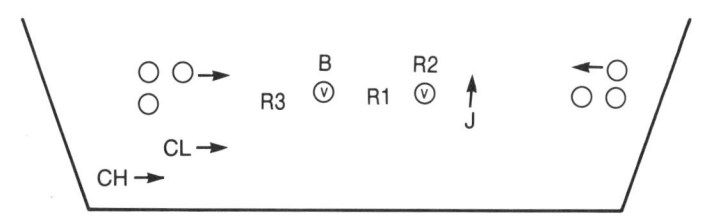

13

(Scene comes to life.)

MR. P (R1): China is a land of nearly 600 million people. In this great country, 1 million souls pass into eternity each month, and the great majority of these have never heard the name of Christ.

(JOHN *pivots out to audience as if entering the room. The others "see" him in offstage focus.)*

J: Excuse me, the door was open, so I came in.

MRS. P (R2) *(stepping off stool):* Are you a new student?

J: Yes, ma'am. My name is John Stam. I'm from Patterson, N.J.

MRS. P: We're so glad you've come. You can meet the rest of the folks after the meeting.

(MRS. P *sits back on her stool and performers lower heads.)*

CL: Betty noticed the tall young man immediately. He was serious about his studies and his concern for missions, yet he could laugh and joke when relaxing.

CH: After several months, John and Betty realized they shared a common concern for China and a growing concern for each other. After one of the Monday meetings, John and Betty began to share their hearts.

(R3 *and* JOHN *kneel as* MR. PAGE *prays. Performers use offstage focus while* CHARLES *and* CLARA *watch scene onstage.)*

MR. P: Lord, again we thank You for each young person here tonight. Lead them into that work which You would have them accomplish. Bless our fellowship and this food, in Thy name we pray, Amen. (R3 *and* JOHN *rise.)* All right, you have about 30 minutes until you must start back to campus. Thank you for coming.

(R3 *and* MR. PAGE *each move a stool back into original position.* R3 *and* MR. AND MRS. PAGE *move to stools leaving,* JOHN *and* BETTY *alone in CS. They speak in offstage focus.)*

J: Betty *(handing Bible to her in pantomimed form in offstage focus)*, you left your Bible in New Testament Survey today.

B: Thank you *(receiving it in offstage pantomime)*, I felt lost without it.

J: Betty, I think it's great that you want to be a missionary . . . I mean, who knows . . . we might end up in the same country or something . . . that is, if I ever make it.

B: I don't understand. Are you having trouble in your classes?

J: No, not that. It's just that my dad has his heart set on me coming back home and helping him with the mission in Patterson. Dad started the mission and all, and he just sort of assumes that God wants me to work there.

B: It would be a great ministry, John. And I'm sure that your dad needs help.

J: Betty, ever since I came to know Christ when I was 15, I've wanted to do God's will. At first, I thought it might be the mission, but the more I study God's Word, the more I feel led to be a foreign missionary. I know there's a need here and in Patterson, but I can't help but feel like somebody can do that who can't go to the foreign field. These Monday nights are great, but they sure do give me mental fits. I just don't know what to do.

B: You know, John, when I decided to be a missionary, I wanted to go to China so bad that I just knew God would send me to Africa. And, only after I finally got rid of my stubborness and said yes to Africa did God say yes to China.

J: Thanks, Betty. You always seem to know what to say . . . Betty, I guess that I'm a little nosey, but I read what you wrote in the back of your Bible.

B: I didn't write that for people to read.

J: I know, Betty . . . but it really spoke to my heart. You see, I, like you, have decided to give all my friends and loves to God.

B: John, I have many friends, but I'll only fall in love once.

J: Well, ah . . . I know that God will give you someone very special, because you deserve the best.

B: Thank you, John. I don't know if God has a husband for me or not. We'll just have to wait and see.

J: Yes, we'll just wait . . . and see.

(JOHN *and* BETTY *keep position but lower heads out of scene.*)

CH: Mr. and Mrs. Page watched the tender romance grow.

CL: But both Betty and John were afraid to fall in love as they so deeply wanted to be sure of God's will. Mrs. Page tells the following story:

(MRS. PAGE [R2] *moves from stool DSC to address audience.*)

My husband and I could see that both of these young people cared a great deal for each other, but as all young couples seeking God's will, they wanted to be sure. This incident was a turning point in their relationship. Betty and John were both strong believers in "healthy body—healthy mind," so, in the early morning, they would each go for a brisk walk along Lake Michigan. One morning, these solo walkers met, and, being sociable, walked together that day. Well, this casual meeting soon became a hoped-for rendezvous. But at about the same time, both of them began to be concerned over the importance this meeting was beginning to have in their lives. Betty came to me and told me that she was just so afraid to do anything that might cause her to miss God's best for her life and ministry so, independent of each other, they curtailed their morning exercise. They continued to see each other casually at school, but no mention of the morning walks was made. However, it was not long before John felt the need for the exercise, so he resumed his walks, heading into a completely different part of the city. Betty, firmly resolved in her decision to put Christ above all relationships, also began her walks again. And so it was that while walking down completely foreign streets, one sidewalk crossed another and around the corner came John and then Betty. How surprised they were at that meeting. But with that meeting, the word "approved" seemed to come from heaven.

(Mrs. Page *moves back to stool.*)

CH: John was a good student at Moody. In fact, one teacher said that he was "a young man of arresting personality and unusual Christian character."

CL: He worked in the missionary union, went street witnessing, and cared for a church in Elida, Ohio.

CH: The 200-mile trip was long, but the blessings of God sustained him in the work of God. However, money was scarce and with the scarcity of money often comes doubt. He told me this story about God's providing hand:

(John *is positioned CS so he "comes alive" and has freedom to move during this speech.*)

J: I had told Tom I was going to ride home with him, but I didn't have any money and couldn't even buy a warm pair of socks for the trip in the car. Then, one night, I pulled on one of the four shirts I had been planning to take home with me, and it ripped. I did not want to take home a mended shirt, for mother would guess that finances were low. I went out by the lake, feeling a bit blue and found myself thinking, "Well, it's all right to trust the Lord, but I wouldn't mind having a few dollars in my pocket." A few minutes later, just as I was crossing Michigan Boulevard, I picked up a five dollar bill from the street. Oh, what a rebuke it was from the Lord. Just one of those gentle rebukes the Lord can so wonderfully give us. The five dollars was beautifully acceptable. The next day I bought a couple of shirts and a good warm pair of socks. These items preach a sermon on the Lord's wonderful power to provide, whatever my future needs may be. (John *should be back in position beside* Betty *when he finishes letter. Bows head out of scene.*)

CL: John and Betty began to date often. Spending their time with Bible reading and prayer . . . seeking God's will. Their love was strong and evident, but there were just too many questions that could not be answered at the moment.

CH: Betty would graduate in April of 1931, but John had another year of school. Betty had been accepted by the China Inland Mission, but John had to wait for graduation and the blessing of his parents. With graduation over, and

Betty's boat to China waiting, the last prayer service at the Page home was difficult for both of them.

(MR. PAGE *moves DSC to stand by* JOHN *and* BETTY. *Offstage focus.*)

MR. P: Well, Betty, how time has flown. Seems as if you just arrived at Moody and now you are graduated, ready to leave for China. We will miss you, won't we, John?

J: Mr. Page, this may surprise you, but Betty and I have grown very fond of each other.

B: Parting is going to be very hard for us, sir.

J: We want to know God's will. I have another whole year of school, and the C.I.M. requires one year on the field before missionary couples can marry. It just wouldn't be fair to Betty to become engaged now because there are so many uncertainties.

MR. P: My dear young friends, as difficult as it may seem, wait on the Lord. Betty, go to China, do that which you know you must do. John, finish school, do that which you know you must do, and God will do what He wills to do. Now, if you'll excuse me, I'll let you say your "good-byes."

(MR. PAGE *moves back to his stool.* JOHN *and* BETTY *are DSC.*)

B: John, I cannot say now all that is in my heart. All I can say is . . . I will miss you greatly. "The Lord watch between me and thee."

J: "The Lord make his face to shine upon thee . . . and give thee" . . . give us both, strength.

(*All performers exit stage. End of act one.*)

ACT TWO

(*All performers come back onstage and are seated on stools with exception of* CLARA *and* CHARLES *who stand in front of their stool.*)

CH: Separation for John and Betty was a time filled with difficulty and heart-searching. But, as often happens in God's work, the fires of testing tempered the steel to new strength.

CL: John buried himself in his work with school, his church, and his missionary training. Betty began her arduous language work in China. Even though she had been raised in China, she had never been exposed to the intricate structure and dialects of the Chinese language.

CH: It took many weeks for a letter to span the ocean that held these two dear ones apart. Away from the physical arms of the man she loved but carried in the arms of the God she served, Betty turned her heart into poetry:

(BETTY *stands directly in front of her stool to speak.*)

> How can I sing, and how pour out my heart,
> When we are half the earth in miles apart?
> There is a Reason; 'Tis our Father's plan
> That draws us each to each, woman and man;
> Yet ties in tender care our love to Him:
> Shall one His work forget, with zeal now dim?
> Never, O Lord! for we would still be true,
> Finishing first what tasks we have to do.
> I love you, Peter—Rock, who are so true,
> Firm and reliable, I trust in you.
> Not above God, and not before His name,
> I love thy dear name next, Beloved John.
> And in His time, and as He wills it so,
> We shall come closer than as yet we know.

(BETTY *sits on stool and bows head.*)

CH: Chosen by his class to present the 1932 graduation address to the Moody Bible Institute, John voiced words of great faith and inspiration on the theme "Bearing Precious Seed."

(JOHN *moves to CS to speak.*)

J: In politics today, men are thinking of international affairs. In business, all the continents are being combed for markets; and even in daily life, every newspaper reader is becoming world-conscious. And yet, we, the people of God, have not fully realized that we are to be a testimony to the world. Heathen populations are growing in numbers daily, but we are not reaching them, much less matching their increasing numbers with increased efforts to bring them the gospel. Not only are heathen populations growing—with the frontiers of civilization moving ahead and education advancing—idolatry and superstition are breaking down. Now is the time to reach men whose minds are swept of old beliefs, before communistic atheism, coming in like a flood, raises other barriers far harder to overcome, and before this generation passes into Christless graves. (*Remains CS and bows head.*)

CL: As John progressed through his senior year in school, the two great questions on his mind were, "What about China and Betty?" and "What about home and father?"

CH: The continual burden for the field expressed by his son, and the moving of the Lord in his own heart, began to soften Mr. Stam, and soon he began to feel earnestly that John should indeed do what God would have him do. Shortly before his graduation, John received his acceptance from the China Inland Mission.

CL: As soon as travel plans had been finalized, John had written Betty at her mission station in Fowyang, but there was no word. The weeks were long, and the mail was silent. Why didn't a letter come? Could Betty have changed her mind? With no idea as to Betty's intentions or her whereabouts in China, John set sail on the Empress of Japan. After a voyage of six weeks, he arrived in Shanghai.

(R3 *becomes* DR. HIRAM *and moves DSC to talk to* JOHN *in offstage focus.*)

DR: Welcome to China, Mr. Stam. Did you have a pleasant crossing?

J: Yes, thank you. I'm sorry, but I don't know your name.

DR: I'm Dr. Hiram, C.I.M. medical doctor in Shanghai. I was in town to pick up some special medicine, so I thought that I would wait for your arrival.

J: Thank you. I trust that no one is seriously ill?

DR: Oh no, not serious but quite uncomfortable . . . a young lady with some tonsilitis. In a few days she'll be back at her station in Fowyang.

(BETTY *was stationed at Fowyang, so* JOHN *is very interested.*)

J: Fowyang! Are there many missionaries at that station?

DR: No, just my patient and the older couple that she works with.

J *(very excitedly)*: The name! What is the name?

DR: Let's see . . . oh yes, "Ferguson." He and his wife have been on the field for almost 30 years.

J: No! . . . the girl's name . . . your patient with the tonsilitis!

DR: Why, she's Dr. Scott's daughter, Betty. Do you know her?

J: Yes, sir! We're . . . old friends. Would it be possible for us to go and visit her?

DR: Why, of course, but perhaps you'd like to do some shopping or sight-seeing first. China is a beautiful land and this city is . . .

J: Excuse me, sir! But there is nothing in the world that I want to do more right now than go and visit your patient. I'll run and get my baggage.

(JOHN *moves back to his stool and* R3 *moves upstage to his stool.*)

CL: And run he did. Ran to the car, just about made Dr. Hiram go off the road, ran to the house, ran past the nurse, and right into the surprised and loving arms of Betty. What a wonderful reunion. Within the next few hours all the questions were answered, all the answers to prayer rejoiced over, all the loneliness expressed, all the love assured of, and then an engagement was announced and a wedding date set.

CH: Yes, that was a wonderful time for them. However, one full year was to transpire before the wedding could take place. Hopefully, this waiting period would deepen their love for the field and their love for each other.

CL: Betty's year was spent in more language training and in working with the women and children near her station. John spent his year in learning the language and in seeing for the first time the great need of the people of China.

CH: Several hundred miles of China separated them, but chains of prayer and love kept them united before the throne of grace. Long before Betty and John went to China, they were keenly aware of the political chaos in that land. The Communists had already kidnapped and murdered several Christian missionaries, but both of these young people felt that the greatest life insurance policy in the world is being in God's will. In a letter mailed to his parents a few weeks before his death, John expressed great faith in God. (JOHN *stands in front of his stool.*)

J: One never knows what one may run into. But we do know that the Lord Jehovah reigns. Above all, don't let anything worry you about us. And so, we can praise God that, for us, everything is well. If we should go on before, it is only the quicker to enjoy the bliss of the Savior's presence, and sooner to be released from the fight against sin and Satan.

CL: Enclosed in this letter was a poem written about the Rev. J. W. Vinson, a missionary who had been martyred by the Communists in China. John said it adequately expressed his and Betty's faith in God.

(JOHN *and* BETTY *stand in front of their stools.*)

J:
>Afraid? Of What?
>To feel the spirit's glad release?
>To pass from pain to perfect peace,
>The strife and strain of life to cease?
>   Afraid—of that?

B:
>Afraid? Of What?
>Afraid to see the Savior's face,
>To hear His welcome, and to trace
>The glory gleam from wounds of grace?
>   Afraid—of that?

J:
>Afraid? Of What?
>A flash, a crash, a pierced heart;
>Darkness, light, O heaven's art!
>A wound of His, a counterpart!
>   Afraid—of that?

BOTH: Afraid? Of What?

B: To do by death what life could not—

J: Baptize with blood a stony plot,

B: Till souls shall blossom from the spot?

BOTH: Afraid—of that?

(JOHN *and* BETTY *sit on stools with heads bowed.* CHARLES *and* CLARA *converse with onstage focus.*)

CL: I'll never forget the wedding. Weren't they a handsome couple?

CH: Yes, Mother, but maybe we're a bit prejudiced.

CL: Such a beautiful day—October 25, 1933. We turned our tennis court into an open-air chapel. The ivy looked like multicolored brown lace as it fluttered in the sunshine of a warm fall afternoon. What a thrill it was to see 140 Chinese Christians witness this wonderful Christian wedding ceremony.

CH: The joy on our children's faces was a stronger testimony to the love of God than months of preaching. The officiating minister was Rev. Reuben A. Torrey, son of the famous evangelist, R. A. Torrey.

(*Performers take indicated position. The organ plays wedding music to cover movement and set mood. Offstage focus.*)

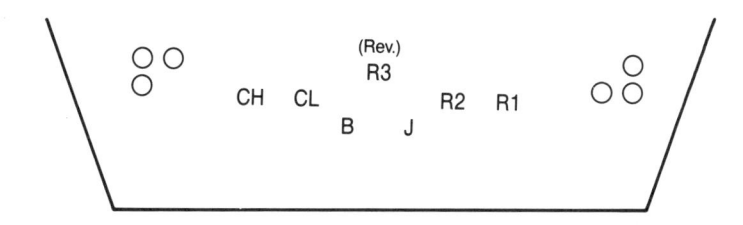

```
            (Rev.)
 o o         R3              o
  o                         o o
     CH  CL        R2  R1
          B  J
```

REV (R3): We are gathered together in the sight of God and this company to join this man and this woman in holy matrimony.

CH (*stepping out of position slightly to address audience*): The sound of these two lovely young dedicated Christians envoking heaven's blessing is still fresh in my mind.

J: I, John Cornelius Stam, take thee, Elisabeth Alden Scott, to be my wedded wife.

B: I, Elisabeth Alden Scott, take thee, John Cornelius Stam, to be my wedded husband. To have an to hold

J: From this day forward,

B: For better—for worse,

J: For richer—for poorer,

B: In sickness and in health,

J: To love and to cherish

(JOHN *and* BETTY *turn to face each other, clasp hands and say*)

BOTH: Till death us do part.

(JOHN *and* BETTY *kneel facing each other. Organ begins to play and soloist sings "O Perfect Love."*)

> O perfect love, all human thought transcending,
> Lowly we kneel in prayer before Thy throne,
> That theirs may be the love which knows no ending,
> Whom thou forevermore dost join in one.

REV: What God hath joined together, let not man put asunder.

(*Full organ on recessional music to cover movement of performers moving back to stools. R2 moves to SL stool this time. R1 and R3 secure swords, but keep them hidden from audience.* JOHN *and* BETTY *stand, turn toward audience, and drop arms and bow heads.*)

CL: Between their wedding at Tsinan and the funeral at Miaosheo were 14 months of happiness. After a honeymoon high in the mountains of Tsingtao, John and Betty began their ministry in Suancheng. John to evangelize and Betty to begin her role as housewife and fellow-laborer.

CH: Sixty miles southwest of Suancheng was a beautiful mountainous region. Here was the town that was to culminate their earthly ministry; the city, Tsingteh.

(JOHN *and* BETTY *come alive, standing CS, speak in offstage focus.*)

B (*as if looking around a room*): It isn't a bad home, John. Oh, it needs a lot of cleaning up, but some hard work and bright curtains and it will be very comfortable.

J: Compared to some homes I visited while at Moody, this is pretty nice. Seems a bit drafty, though.

B: We must do something about that. If we put a small coal stove near the doorway of our bedroom, it will also warm this small adjacent room.

J: I don't think that we can really afford to heat both rooms. Coal is scarce and so is money.

B (*coyly*): John, I'm afraid that it's either heat both rooms or . . . put the . . . crib in our room.

J (*blankly*): The crib? (*Look of question grows to one of understanding and excitement.*) Betty! When did you find out? Why didn't you tell me sooner? Here, sit down, you need to rest!

B: I feel just fine. There's no need for a fuss. Our new little houseguest should arrive in September.

J: C'mon, Betty, show me just where you think that stove should go. (BETTY *and* JOHN *remain in CS and bow heads.*)

CL: And thus it was that on September 11, 1934, Betty presented John with a beautiful baby girl, Helen Priscilla.

CH: Rumors of the ever-present Communists were always abounding. Like dawn fog, the red bandits would sweep across a Chinese hamlet, stealing, killing, and kidnapping the ever-valuable Europeans and Americans. Ransom was a vital source of revenue in the diet of the Communists. Ever since the 1917 Bolshevik revolution in Russia, a Communist faction had warred in China. John and Betty knew the conditions of the land to which they ministered; the potential gain, and also the potential pain. But they came at God's bidding. John did all that was humanly possible to insure the safety of his wife and family. Only when he had received full assurance from the district magistrate that the city of Tsingteh was safe from Communist attack, did John move to that city.

CL: But in his heart, John knew that danger was ever present. He knew that the whole of China was a field, like a field of rice. While he and Betty sought to harvest the field for God, Satan had his workers in the field. They knew that each day was a gift from God, a gift to be lived to its fullest. While in China, John wrote out a devotional for some students. In it, he said:

J: Let us consider the passage in John, chapter 12, which says, "Except a grain of wheat fall into the ground and die, it abideth alone: but if it die, it bringeth forth much fruit." Christ said, "For this cause came I unto this hour, Father, glorify thy name." In our own lives it is well to remember that God's supervision is so blessedly true that at any given moment we may stop, and whether we face suffering or joy, we may say, "For this cause came I unto this hour."

CH: The date was December 6, 1934.

(R2 *runs DSC to warn of attack.* JOHN *and* BETTY *"come alive" as soon as* R2 *begins to speak. Onstage focus is used for opening of this scene.*)

GIRL (R2): Mr. Stam! Mr. Stam! We must leave . . . Communists have just attacked our city.

B: John! What will we do, what will happen?

J: We must not panic. That will only hurt our efforts. *(To girl)* Get Helen ready to travel . . . take as little as possible.

GIRL: I will pack food for the little one.

(R3 *comes alive and pivots off of stool and comes to far DSR. He points to missionary house in offstage focus. See diagram.*)

SOL 1 (R3): Hurry! Down this street! The missionaries live in that house.

B: John! They're here!

J *(placing right arm around* BETTY *and* GIRL *stands to his left)*: Father, protect us, Thy children, if it be Thy will. We trust in Your divine care; O God! protect Helen!

(R1 *comes alive and pivots off of stool and comes to far DSL. He speaks to them in offstage focus.*)

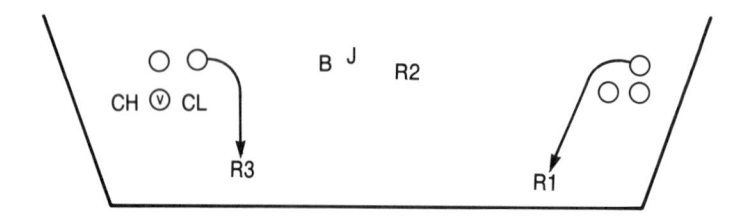

```
\           O O         B  J            O  \
 \          CH Ⓥ CL         R2        O O  \
  \              ↓                    ↙     \
   \            R3                  R1       \
```

SOL 2 (R1): Your house is surrounded! There is no escape!

J: We have no money. Take what you want but . . .

SOL 1: Silence! You are prisoners!

SOL 2: Your house and all it contains are now confiscated by the People's Army.

(*Soldiers pivot military fashion and move US past* JOHN *and* BETTY. *R2 exits scene. They position facing into wings on each side of couple with back to couple, as if they were on guard duty.* JOHN *and* BETTY *bow heads and remain CS.*)

CH: While being held prisoner, John sent the first letter, containing the ransom demand, to the China Inland Mission.

(JOHN *comes alive and faces audience.*)

J: Dear Brethren:
My wife, baby, and I are today in the hands of the communists in the city of Tsingteh. Their demand is $20,000 for our release. All our possessions and stores are in their hands, but we praise God for peace in our hearts and a meal tonight. God grant you wisdom in what you do, and us fortitude, courage, and peace of heart. He is able—and a wonderful Friend in such a time. The Lord bless and guide you, and as for us, may God be glorified whether by life or by death. (*Bows head.*)

CH: The Communist army of 6,000 now controlled the entire district and on December 7, they moved on to the city of Miaosheo. Through a miracle, Helen was allowed to live and remain with her parents. A second letter came from John, adding:

J: I tried to persuade them to let my wife and baby go back with a letter to you, but they wouldn't let her, and so we both made the trip to Miaosheo today. They want $20,000, which we have told them we are sure cannot be paid. God give you wisdom in what you do and give us grace and fortitude. He is able.

(*Soldiers each carry a stool to CS and then return to guard position.* JOHN *and* BETTY *move back to sit on stools.*)

```
              R1    B  J      R3      R2
          O   O────▶O  O  ◀────         O
       CH O   CL                       O O
```

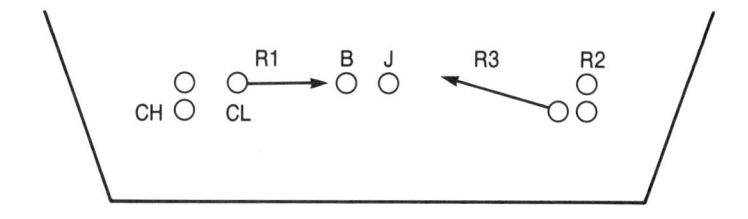

CH: That night, John, Betty, and Helen Priscilla were locked in a back room of a large Chinese mansion that had been looted by the Communists. The Red army was impatient to move on. The soldiers were grumbling that no money would come. John and Betty knew that this might be their last night on earth. Those few hours were sacred for these young heroes of the faith.

(JOHN *and* BETTY *come alive and perform this scene with onstage focus. All physical action is done in proper pantomime form.*)

B: I can't loosen the rope; it's tied too tightly!

J: Try a nail file. Isn't there one in your purse?

B: The last guard took my bag just before he locked the door!

J: Well . . . I guess that my hands won't be hurting for long anyway . . .

(BETTY *places her arms around him and lays her head upon his breast.*) Do you remember studying the deaths of the apostles in missions?

B: It all sounded rather heroic as I remember . . .

J: I could always see the wicked, taunting crowd and right in the center was the noble Christian tied to a stake . . . or a cross . . . and he was always smiling boldly into the face of death. And all the wicked people in the crowd were so impressed with his courage. But for some reason, I don't feel very brave.

B: Honey, there's no shame in that. And we have followed God . . . even to this.

J: We've only been married 14 months . . .

B: And they've been good months, John. We've had more happiness in 14 months than some couples have in a lifetime. Oh . . . Helen's awake. Shh . . . don't cry. (BETTY *moves off stool and kneels to the left of her stool as if she is looking in the cradle.*)

J: Keep her still . . . if the guards hear her crying, they'll . . .

B (*looking at the baby*): She'll be fine. Doesn't know anything is wrong in the world. As long as she is dry and fed . . . everything is all right. What are we going to do with her . . . The guards will get angry again, I know it. (*Fear grows in her as she thinks of what may happen.*) Why did they want to kill a baby? How could anyone be so hateful?

J: She's a "foreign devil" like her parents. *(Thoughtfully)* There will not be another Mr. Chi Loo to die for our baby.

B: I was stunned when that guard grabbed Helen . . . he was going to shoot her. My heart just stopped. All I heard was the shot and then saw Mr. Loo on the ground.

J: He dared the soldier to shoot him and not the baby. Mr. Loo was one of the first Chinese to trust Christ in this province. His wife was killed two months ago . . . now, he is with her. Betty, aren't you a little afraid?

B: Afraid of when it happens, yes, but not afraid of dying. Laying in that hospital bed for three months made me realize so strongly how much I need the strength of God. This is His will . . . I do know that *(Helen has fallen asleep)*. There . . . see, she's asleep. She is such a good baby.

J: You know, love, she looks more and more like you. *(To baby)* What does the future hold for you, Helen? Will you ever have the chance to write poetry like your mama?

B: What can we do with her? All the money we planned to bribe the guards with is gone . . . it was in the lining of the diaper bag . . . I never thought they'd take that . . .

(SOLDIER 1 *moves DS past* JOHN *and* BETTY *and speaks out toward audience addressing other soldiers.*)

SOL 1: I will get the Americans. Call the villagers to the top of that hill. This should make an impression on them. *(Freeze.)*

J *(resolutely)*: The guards are coming. Put her into the sleeping bag and zip it up. In the confusion, maybe they'll forget that she is here.

B: But what if she cries . . . she could suffocate in that bag!

J: We have no other choice. There are believers in this village, but if the Communists find them now . . . they'll kill them. You know that! All we can do is try and hide her and pray that the Christians will come and find her after the Communists are gone.

B: John . . . I can't do that! I can't abandon her . . . There must be something else that we can do . . . We've got to . . .

J: There is nothing else that we can do, Betty! *(Pleadingly)* You have to use that faith of yours . . . You have to *(praying and looking up as* BETTY *slumps against his side and holds her baby)* O dear God. Please, take care of this child . . . We are ready . . . and willing . . . to die for the name of Christ . . . but . . . oh, dear God . . . in Your mercy and power . . . please spare' the life of this baby . . .

J: They're coming . . . do it.

(BETTY *picks up and holds the baby.*)

Do it!! Put her in the bag and zip it up. Be sure and fold the end up over the top so it looks empty.

B: Helen *(looking into the face of her baby)*, I love you, darling . . . *(looking to heaven)* God . . . here's my baby. Please protect her . . .

J: Hurry . . . they're coming . . .

B *(places baby in bag and zips it up)*: Good-by, dear Helen. God watch you . . . God watch you.

(SOLDIER 2 *moves out DSR and addresses* JOHN *and* BETTY *in offstage focus.*)

SOL 2: Get up . . . come with us. Leave your belongings.

(SOL 2 *draws a knife,* JOHN *turns his back to audience, and* SOL 2 *cuts* JOHN'S *ropes in offstage focus as SOL 1 speaks.*)

SOL 1: You villagers, watch and see what happens to those who oppose us.

SOL 2: Death to the American Christian spies. Kneel!

(JOHN *and* BETTY *kneel together; both facing audience.*)

SOL 1: May all the enemies of the people be as these.

SOL 2: Death will forever silence these foreign devils and their foreign God.

(Soldiers turn to face each other, directly in front of JOHN *and* BETTY. *They draw swords, cross them over the heads of* JOHN *and* BETTY, *and bring them down forcefully. As the blades pass in front of the couple, they should stiffen their bodies visibly, and then slightly slump. The use of real swords is imperative to gain desired effect. If possible, dim lights so that only one spot is on the kneeling couple and the two soldiers. The scene freezes as organ plays softly and as the soloist sings the final line of "O Perfect Love."*)

SOLOIST: Whom Thou forever more dost join in one.

(Stage blackout so that all performers except CHARLES *and* CLARA *may leave the stage area.* CHARLES *and* CLARA *are standing CS when spotlight comes up on them.*)

CH: None of the Chinese dared to move the bodies of these fallen heroes. Many hours after their death, the sun set, and a cold winter wind swept the bloodstained knoll. With the coming of the new day, the momentary absence of the communists, and the arrival of some Chinese Christians, a simple funeral service was held. Murdered by Chinese Communists, their graves were watered by the tears of Chinese Christians. After the service, a Chinese couple inspected the home where John and Betty had been held captive, and there, warm and without concern, Helen Priscilla was found bundled in her sleeping bag. Apart from needing fresh clothing and food, the dear little girl was as healthy as could be.

CL: Left alone for 30 hours, the angels had taken good care of our little granddaughter. After a difficult and miraculous trip through China, Helen was brought to us.

CH: The miracle child lived and prospered just as did the work for which her parents died. The Communists had killed two of the finest, most noble, young Christians who ever left American shores, but the will of God was done.

CL: We have received letters from every continent and dozens of countries expressing sympathy, yes, but much more than this, letters telling of young men and women who have surrendered their lives to Christ. Entire schools have been fired to live for God through the tragedy of our children. God's perfect will was done.

CH: Clara, I've closed the letter with this thought: As families and as a station, we wish to bear testimony that our faith in God has been strengthened. While Jesus Christ calls upon all who would be truly His to deny himself and to take up his cross and follow Him, yet the cross that He fits to our shoulders is joyously endurable in view of the comfort of His sustaining grace.

CL: Yes, dear, His sustaining grace. May the lives of our children be the means of sharing with others the wonder of God's sustaining grace.

CH: Clara and I pray that each of you will come to know a richer life in Christ because of what happened to our dear ones. They were privileged to die for Him, but to us is given the responsibility of living for Him. As Betty wrote in her Bible, "To me to live is Christ, and to die is gain."

(Spotlights dim as CHARLES *and* CLARA *leave the stage.)*

BRIDGE OF BLOOD

Jim Elliot Takes Christ to the Aucas

Cast:
ELISABETH: *narrator of the play*
JIM: *Elisabeth's husband*
R1: *male who portrays: Nate Saint, student body president*
R2: *female who portrays: Marj Saint, Mrs. Shuell*
R3: *male who portrays: Pete Fleming, college student*
R4: *female who portrays: Olive Fleming, Miriam Shuell*
R5: *male who portrays: Ed McCully, Wayne, Mr. Shuell*
R6: *female who portrays: Marilou McCully, Dayuma*
R7: *male who portrays: Roger Youderian, preacher*
R8: *female who portrays: Barbara Youderian*

This cast list is the recommended assignment of parts. If a larger cast is desired, simply divide the parts further.

Props:
metal stools for each cast member

Sound Notes:
Organ music is needed. "Nothing Between My Soul and My Saviour" is recommended, as well as "Be Still, My Soul."

Stage Arrangement:
Diagrams appear throughout the script indicating actors' positions. The following symbols are used:

- ○ —stools
- △ —actor's back to audience
- ▽ —actors facing audience
- ↑↓ —actors move as per direction arrows. Also indicates how stools are moved.

Bridge of Blood, written and directed by David H. Robey, premiered in Phillips Chapel on the campus of Tennessee Temple Schools during the summer of 1973. It featured Faith Himes, David H. Robey, Curtis Cooper, Judy Hale, Pat Gray, Edward Flanagan, Jackie Chrest, Stephen Marshall, Sharon Cooper, Lloyd Smith III, Debbie Williams.

(Blackout—the five men seat themselves on the stools along the upstage part of the platform. They have their backs to the audience. The narrator stands DSC and comes alive when the stage lights come up.)

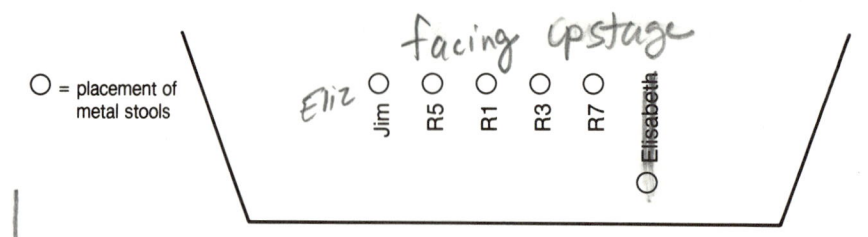

ELISABETH: Thirty-two years* seems like a long time, and it is a long time for the living, but for the dead, merely a pause between moments of eternity. Thirty-two years* ago last January, God took my husband, Jim Elliot, home to heaven. Jim, along with four other missionary men, met death in the form of Auca lances on a muddy sandbar along the Curaray River in Central Ecuador. The world called it a purposeless nightmare of tragedy, but a lost and dying world could never understand Jim's creed: "He is no fool who gives what he cannot keep to gain what he cannot lose." The waves of the river quickly erased these missionaries' footprints from the sandy beach along its shores, but the waves of time cannot, and must not, erase the memory of these men from the hearts and minds of God's people. These men gave their lives for God's purpose with, as my Jim would say, "reckless abandon to the will of God." Not all the saints were present at Pentecost, nor were they martyred by the pagan Roman emperors, for these men who gave their lives to form the "Bridge of Blood" to the Aucas were saints in the fullest meaning of the word. Jim Elliot, Pete Fleming, Ed McCully, Nate Saint, and Roger Youderian died serving their living Christ. Tonight, I tell you their story with the prayer that it may better prepare you to live, and perhaps die, serving the Lord Jesus Christ.

ELISABETH: Jim Elliot was born in Portland, Oreg., in 1927, the third child of Fred and Clara Elliot. Jim accepted Christ at an early age, as did all the Elliot children. Jim was only six when one night he spoke to his mother about his salvation experience.

(JIM comes alive, pivots on stool, and faces audience.)

JIM: Now, Mama, the Lord Jesus can come whenever He wants to. He could take our whole family now because I'm saved.

(JIM keeps face toward audience but lowers head and is out of scene.)

ELISABETH: Through high school, Jim kept a very firm testimony. Being quite an extrovert, as well as a successful athlete, Jim was well-known among the students. But Jim never dropped his testimony to win popularity: Christ and biblical principles always came first.

(*Note: This date should be changed according to the time span between January 1956, and the date the performance is given. ELISABETH moves from center stage to her stool DSL before speaking.)

(*Cafeteria sketch*—JIM *carries stool DSR and is seated as* R5 *student comes from the men on the stools and carries his stool and places it beside* JIM. *This man becomes the student "Wayne." Offstage focus is used.*)

R5: Hey, Jim! What ya' got for lunch?

JIM: Same as usual; protein dieter's special: (*Pantomime of removing food from lunch bag*) One peanut butter sandwich, two oatmeal cookies, and an apple. Say, what are you doing on Friday night?

R5: Nothing, as far as I know, why?

JIM: How'd you like to help me take my Sunday School class roller skating?

R5: Well, (*fumbling for words of excuse*) . . . I don't know . . . Homework! I've got an awful lot of homework to do. (*Sees someone approaching in offstage focus.*) Say! here comes Mr. Student Body President. (*Impressed.*) Wonder what he wants?

(R1 *doubles as student body president and stands behind and between stools on which* JIM *and* R5 *are seated.*)

R1: Hello, Jim . . . Wayne. How's everything?

R5: Real good, Bob!

R1: Say, I hope you guys have made the right kind of plans for Friday night.

R5: What's going on Friday night?

R1: The all-school dance. Just about the biggest dance of the year and I have your tickets right here, so if you'll just pay me I'll . . .

JIM (*cutting in*): You don't have my ticket!

R1: What do you mean? Don't tell me that your . . .

R5 (*cutting in*): Oh (*embarrassed at conflict*), I just remembered, Jim and I are taking his Sunday School class roller skating.

R1: You can do that any time, but this dance only comes once a year.

JIM: Roller skating isn't the only reason I'm not going to your dance. I'm a Christian and the spirit of Christ lives in me. Wherever I go, I take Christ with me, and I'm not taking Christ to one of your dances.

R1: Listen Jim, if you don't buy a ticket, a lot of the other guys won't either, and the student body needs the money. We all have to support the school, and you're just as much a part of this student body as I am.

JIM: You're right in that I'm in the student body, but not the way you are! Christ put me in the world to live for Him, and not to become a part of the world. And that's why I'm not going to your dance!

(R1 *and* R5 *with stool move back to original position—*JIM *remains with head down, out of scene.*)

ELISABETH: In 1945, Jim enrolled in Wheaton College, intent upon the task of pleasing his Lord. Jim sought out friends that he knew would help him to grow spiritually. With some of these friends, he developed habits that would have a strong influence in shaping his life. During his freshman year, he wrote his father of life in the dormitory.

(JIM *comes alive and faces the audience—remains seated on stool.*)

JIM: Several of my housemates and I have begun to have prayer together here in our den, and such times we do have. The firstfruits of glory itself! As soon as we hit upon a subject that has a need for God to fill, we dive for our knees and tell Him about it. These are the times I'll remember about college when all the philosophy has slipped out memory's back gate. God is still on the throne and we're still on His footstool, and there's only a knee's distance between. (*Lowers head.*)

ELISABETH: During my freshman year at school, I became acquainted with this man who was to become so much of my life. Some students seemed to regard Jim as a spiritual extremist because of his seriousness of daily studies and his walk with God. You see, Jim never thought of "today" as an entity in itself, but only as it would play a part in building "tomorrow." While at Wheaton, Jim began a journal that now reveals his deepest thoughts from those days. Kept up until his death, the last few pages of the journal were found scattered among the sticks and leaves on that sandbar along the Curaray River. The intense desire to win souls coupled with a total abandon to serve Christ, pointed Jim to the mission field. Hardship, sacrifice, and even death, are not uncommon among missionaries, but this did not deter Jim from seeking to do God's will. In his journal, he wrote:

JIM (*comes alive*): God, I pray Thee, light these idle sticks of my life and may I burn up for Thee. Consume my life, my God, for it is Thine. I seek not a long life but a full one, like Yours, Lord Jesus. (*Lowers head.*)

ELISABETH: Certain student elements told Jim that he was making a big mistake in considering some lonely mission field. After all, they reasoned, shouldn't a man of such great speaking ability stay in the States and minister to those who could most appreciate his value?

(*College student sketch—*R3 *doubles as student and comes to stand beside* JIM. *Offstage focus used.*)

R3: Jim, wasn't that startling what the chapel speaker said today? The youth of America are a neglected mission field!

JIM: Of their own doing for the most part. Having a radio, they turn off the gospel message. Old family Bibles do little but fill up a bookshelf.

R3: Don't be so negative. Think of the numbers of young people who could be

32

encouraged to come to Christ if someone, such as yourself, Jim, would dedicate his talents to the task. There are many large churches willing to pay good salaries to talented college graduates who will come and minister to their young people.

JIM: Agreed, there is a lot of work that needs to be done in America, but a life of baby-sitting a bunch of spoiled delinquents for some big church isn't the kind of work that I want to do. God hasn't called me to that.

R3: How do you know? Show me the verse where God called you to go to some dirt village and waste your life on a handful of Indians. Saul received his call on the road to Damascus when he saw a bright light. When did you see your bright light?

JIM: Saul didn't have a New Testament. Our young men are going into professional fields because they don't feel "called" to the mission field. We don't need a call, we need a kick in the pants. We must begin thinking in terms of going out and stop our weeping because they won't come in. Who wants to step into an igloo? The tombs themselves are not colder than are most of our fundamental churches. May God send us forth.

(JIM *lowers head* and R3 *moves back to his original position.*)

ELISABETH: Through careful searching of the scriptures and much prayer, Jim answered God's leading to work among the Quichua Indians in Ecuador. This was a decision arrived at only after four years of college in which he carefully sought God's will. Jim's parents were understandably very concerned over Jim's future. Already, one of their sons had gone to Peru as a missionary, and parental love was very strong. In a loving and fiery letter to his parents, Jim wrote: *(comes alive and faces audience.)*

JIM: I do not wonder that you are saddened at the word of my going to South America. This is nothing else than what the Lord Jesus warned us of when He told the disciples that they must become so infatuated with the Kingdom and following Him that all other allegiances must become as though they were not. And He never excluded the family tie. In fact, those loves which we regard as closest, He told us must become as hate in comparison with our desires to uphold His cause. Grieve not, then, if your sons seem to desert you, but rejoice, seeing the will of God done gladly. I dare not stay home while Quichuas perish. (JIM *carries stool back to original position and sits with back to audience.*)

ELISABETH: Jim and I continued to write, sharing our thoughts and then gradually our hearts, but we did not marry until October of 1953, as we both felt that our lives with God must come before our lives with each other. Jim felt the need to travel with a man who could help in this pioneer missionary work and he earnestly prayed for God to fill this need. Pete Fleming, a friend of Jim's for many years, had also felt an increasing burden for missions, and he and Jim prayed for God's guidance in the possibility of their going to Ecuador together. A Dr. Tidmarsh, missionary to Ecuador, had corresponded with both Jim and Pete and was able to visit them while in the States on furlough. When he returned to Ecuador, Pete wrote him and told him of God's working in his life.

(R3 *moves to CS and faces audience.*)

R3: Since your visit I have been very much in prayer about going to Ecuador. Jim and I have exchanged several letters in which I told him of the increased desire to go forth, and of the scriptures that God seemingly had brought to mind to confirm it. "He that taketh not up his cross after me is not worthy of me," "He that loveth father or mother more than me is not worthy of me," "He that findeth his life shall lose it; and he that loseth his life for My sake shall find it." This door seems to be the Lord's answer to my prayers. (*Lowers head.*)

ELISABETH: Pete and Jim left for Quito, Ecuador, on February 4, 1952. The first task at hand was language school, and both men began this hurdle with energy. While in school, they sought to find out all they could about the primitive tribes of Indians that inhabited the jungles of Ecuador. It is impossible to study these remote tribes for very long without coming across the name of the Aucas. From the reports of hunters, oil companies, and friendly Indians, a picture of an intelligent, cunning, and fairly industrious people emerged. But the picture also revealed deeply rooted hatred of intruders and great spiritual darkness. Pete and Jim spoke often of the Auca problem and prayed that if it be God's will, they might be the ones to take Christ to the Aucas. In his diary, Pete wrote (*comes alive*):

R3: I am longing to reach the Aucas. The thought scares me at times, but I am ready. I would gladly give my life for that tribe if only to see an assembly of those proud, clever, smart people gathering around a table to honor the Son—gladly, gladly! What more could be given to life? (R3 *returns to original position.*)

ELISABETH: We now have two of our missionaries on the field. The third man is Ed McCully. Ed was also a Wheaton grad who, upon graduation in the spring of 1950, enrolled in law school. He took a job as a night-clerk in a hotel so that he could have time to study at night. But instead, he began to spend more and more time in studying his Bible. On September 22, 1950, he wrote Jim and told him of the Lord's dealing with him. (R5 *takes CS.*)

R5: Since taking this job, things have happened. Each night the Lord seemed to get hold of me a little more. Night before last I was reading in Nehemiah. I finished the book and read it through again. Here was a man who left everything, as far as position was concerned, to go and do a job. And because he went, the whole remnant back in Jerusalem got right with the Lord. Jim, I couldn't get away from it. The Lord was dealing with me. On the way home yesterday morning, I took a long walk and came to a decision. I have one desire now—to live for the Lord, putting all my energy and strength into it. Maybe He'll send me someplace where the name of Jesus Christ is unknown. Jim, I'm taking the Lord at His word, and trusting Him to prove His word. Well, that's it. Two days ago I was a law student. Today I'm an untitled nobody. Thanks, Jim, for intercession on my behalf. Don't let up. *(Lowers head.)*

ELISABETH: After dropping out of law school, Ed enrolled in the School of Missionary Medicine in Los Angeles, where he spent a year of intensive study. Following God's leading every step of the way, he and his wife, Marilou, and eight-month-old Stevie, set sail for Ecuador on December 10, 1952. Shortly after their arrival, Ed visited Jim and Pete at their mission station called Shandia. After returning to Quito, he wrote his parents *(comes alive):*

R5: I have just spent 12 days in the jungles with Jim Elliot and Pete Fleming among the lowland Quichua Indians. If the Lord permits, we hope to locate there in a few months. During these days, many incredible sights came to my eyes: the endless line of people seeking medical aid, the weird chant of witchcalling, the helpless cry of the death mourners. I praise God for bringing us to this land to work with these people. I pray that we might be faithful to our calling.

(R5 moves back to original position.)

ELISABETH: Because of the extremely dense jungles of Ecuador, a few miles separating mission outposts could mean a few days of travel. The coming of the missionary pilot was truly a great boon to these remote outposts, and one of the best pilots was Nate Saint. Born in 1923 into a strict and loving family of fundamental Christians, Nate had a boyhood of discipline and Bible training. As a 13-year-old boy he accepted Christ as his personal Savior at a Christian camp.

Nate's boyhood was marked by two powerful happenings: at the age of seven he had a plane ride. That plane ride awakened in him a yearning to fly that would lead him to his life's work. Also, he was stricken with the crippling disease, osteomyletis, which left his right leg permanently scarred. Repeated attempts to get into the military air corps were always stymied when Nate's osteomyletis wounds were discovered. Frustration and indecision plagued him relentlessly. Stationed in Detroit as a flight mechanic, Nate often attended the Zoller Gospel Tabernacle, where the preaching of the Word continually prodded his sensitive heart.

(NATE SAINT *church sketch*)

("Nothing Between My Soul and the Saviour" is either played on organ or piano to cover movement of cast or else the cast sings one verse of the song. ELISABETH *does*

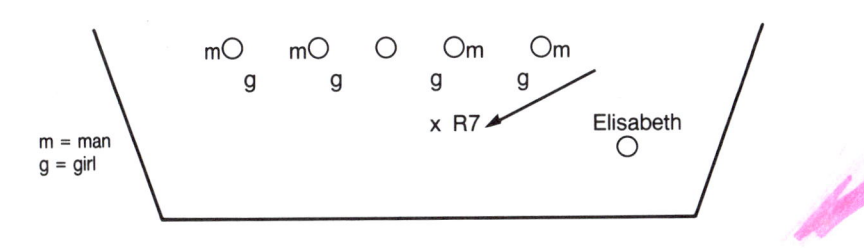

not sing as she watches the action of the cast. The cast gets in position and listens to the "preacher" speak with offstage focus. Check diagram.)

R7: Can you sing the words of this song with a clear heart before God? Is there really nothing between your will and God's will? Please, let go of the past and claim a future with Christ. Lord *(cast bows head during prayer)*, grant Thy blessing on us and keep us from sin. Amen.

(Song is played again to cover movement. JIM, R3, R7 return to stools. R6 and R8 exit. R2 and R4 double as MRS. SHUELL and MIRIAM. R5 doubles for MR. SHUELL.)

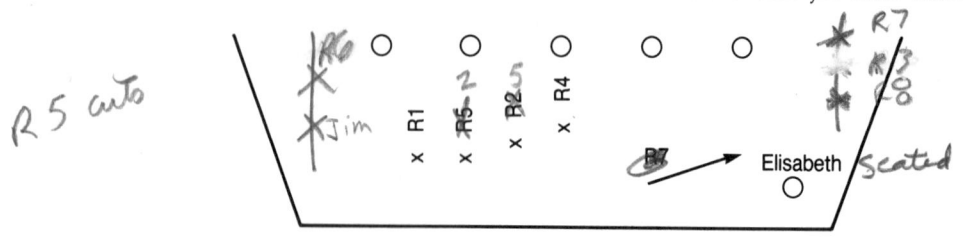

R5: Excuse me, young man. My name is Albert Shuell. This is my wife and my daughter, Miriam.

R1: How do you do, sir! I'm Nate Saint. I surely do appreciate your church services.

R2: We're so glad to have you come. I've seen you here often and couldn't help but notice that you always come alone. It must be lonely for a serviceman to be away from home for so long.

R1: Yes, ma'am . . . it is. But, I manage, I guess.

R2: Do you think there's any possibility that you might come home for Sunday dinner with us? We have plenty to eat!

R1: Thank you very much. I'd surely enjoy that. It's been a long time since I've been in a home.

R2: Well, then, we'd better hurry, or that roast may be part charcoal.

(Group stays where they are and lower heads.)

ELISABETH: And so began a brief, but close friendship between this young man and a godly family. Miriam was strongly attracted to Nate and prayed diligently that Nate would let God have his life. Miriam belonged to a Christian club and Nate occasionally attended meetings with her.

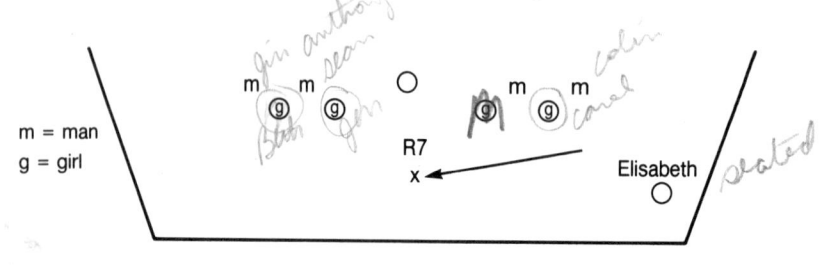

36

(Club sketch—readers sit on or stand by stools along the back of stage but leave center clear for R7 and R4. Cast listens to testimony with offstage focus.)

R7: And now, Miriam Shuell will give the devotional. She told me that she's a little nervous but I know she'll do a fine job. C'mon up here, Miriam.

(R7 exits CS as R4 comes to speak facing audience.)

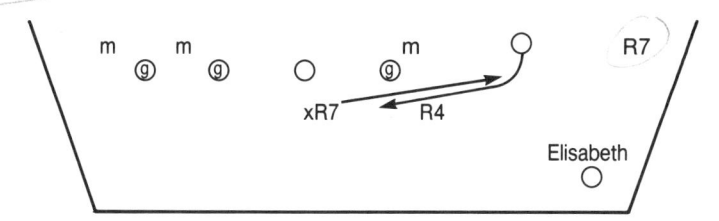

```
    m     m          m         R7
    ⓖ     ⓖ    ○    ⓖ    ○
                xR7 ← R4
                          Elisabeth
                             ○
```

R4: I'm not a woman preacher . . . in fact, I'm scared to death, but I really am thankful for the opportunity to share my heart with you. Believe it or not, I did have a fairly good sermonette planned, but I feel that God would just have me give my testimony. I guess that God wants me to talk with you and not preach at you, so I'll just tell you what God has done for me.

First of all, He saved me by His grace. When a friend gives you a wonderful gift, you usually try to find a way to give a gift in return. I have nothing of earthly value to give God so . . . I have given Him my life. Sometimes I imagine that a roaring fire is burning up a great house. And when all the walls, floors, and roofs are gone, only a few precious stones will remain. I guess my life is like that. Someday I'll see Jesus face to face and all my good works and so-called virtues will burn up just like that house, and all that will be left are the souls that God has brought to Himself through me. The way I figure it, I've only got about 70 years at the most to thank God for something that He did for me that will last for eternity. Because God commanded us to go and because I want to serve Him, I've decided to give my life to God for mission work. I don't know where I'm going, but I do know who's leading the way. I guess that's all I have to say.

(All women except ELISABETH leave stage. All men sit on stools with backs to audience except R1 who is facing audience with head down until he speaks.)

ELISABETH: Nate felt this testimony very deeply, and the Spirit of God led him to yield his life to full-time Christian service. In a letter to a friend, Nate described the circumstances and results of this testimony service.

(R1 comes alive and moves DSC.)

R1: As soon as I could, I stepped out of the building to get away from people and things, so that I could see what the deal was. As I walked, I prayed to God and gave Him everything I had. A joy, such as I had never known since the night I accepted Jesus' forgiveness of sins, seemed to leave me almost weak with gratitude. I was completely relaxed and happy. The old life of chasing things that are of a temporal sort seemed so absolutely insane, once the Lord had shown me the new plan. Before this, I had no idea of the real truth of the statement, "He that loveth his life shall lose it." Now it seems quite clear. *(Lowers head.)*

ELISABETH: In a letter to his mother, he again shared his new calling, telling his desire to serve and foreshadowing his going to the Aucas.

(R1 comes alive.)

R1: I've always believed that if the Lord wanted a guy in full-time service on the mission field, He would make him unbearably miserable in the pursuit of any other end. So, methinks, the aircraft industry has suffered the loss of a "big operator," and the Lord has won for Himself a "li'l operator." The Lord has given me no desire to preach, but I'd like someday to be able to tell somebody who has never heard. Please pray that I'll be kept from useless side tracks.

(Returns to stool.)

ELISABETH: Nate immediately began to search for openings of service in various mission fields, thinking that God had led him to abandon his aviation training. A letter from his father told him of the newly-formed Missionary Aviation Fellowship, and God's hand led him to this organization. In November of 1945 he met Marjorie Farris, a registered nurse, and in 1948, they were married on Valentine's Day. They had already answered the call to missions individually before they agreed to go as a couple. September of 1948 found the Saints busily setting up housekeeping at Shell Mera, an abandoned Shell Oil Company outlet that had a fairly intact airfield. Thus Nate Saint had also taken up his mission work in the jungles of Ecuador.

The final member of our missionary band is Roger Youderian. Born in 1924, Rog was raised by a devout and loving Christian mother. However, it wasn't until 1944 that he was saved, while working as a chaplain's assistant in the European theater of the war. In December of 1944, he wrote his mother:

(R7 comes to life and moves DSC to speak to audience.)

R7: The happiest day of my life was the day I accepted Jesus Christ as my Savior for the remission of my sins, duly repented for, and with God's help I hope and pray for the faith and strength to glorify our Father through my daily living as a witness and follower of Christ. I used to say, "this is a great world." With this new faith, this feeling has increased a thousand fold, and I fairly ache within from happiness and rejoicing in sharing God's manifold blessing which He gives to this world with infinite mercy and grace. *(Lowers head.)*

ELISABETH: Less than 10 months later, the yielded young man expressed his willingness to follow God's leading into full-time service. *(R7 comes alive.)*

R7: I've a secret to tell you, Mother. In this, more than anything in the world, I want the action to precede the announcement. Ever since I accepted Christ as my personal Savior last fall, I've felt the call to either missionary or ministerial work after my release from the service. Can't say now what the calling will be, but I want to be a witness for Him and live following Him every second of my life. (*R7 returns to original position.*)

ELISABETH: Rog enrolled at the Northwestern Schools in Minneapolis and took mission courses. While there, he met and married Barbara Orton. In 1953, they set out with their six-month-old Beth Elaine for Ecuador. The Lord nurtured their interest in this field through the testimony of Frank and Marie Drown, missionaries to the head-hunting Jivaro Indians of Ecuador.

At this point in the story, the men, with their wives and families, are all busy on the field. All on separate outposts, the only links to civilization and each other were the shortwave radio and the yellow plane of Nate Saint. The men had often talked and prayed about the possibility of reaching the Aucas for Christ, but being primarily a nomadic people, the Aucas were almost impossible to locate. However, the prayers of the missionaries germinated on September 19, 1955. While flying a regular air mission, Nate made an unexpected and remarkable discovery. That night, a special prayer meeting was called at the Saint home: Jim Elliot, Nate Saint, Ed McCully, Roger Youderian, and Pete Fleming met to discuss the subject that would decide their destinies.

(*R1 and R3 come alive, pivot out to audience, stay seated on stools, and converse with offstage focus. Other men remain in back position until they speak.*)

R3: C'mon, Nate. What's the meeting for? Why all the mystery?

R1: I don't want to say anything until we're all here.

R3: You sure know how to build suspense. I wish the others would hurry up and get here!

R1: There's the door. C'mon in! It's open!

(JIM, *R5, and R7 pivot out to audience and join the scene as if entering through a door. Note focus lines on diagram.*)

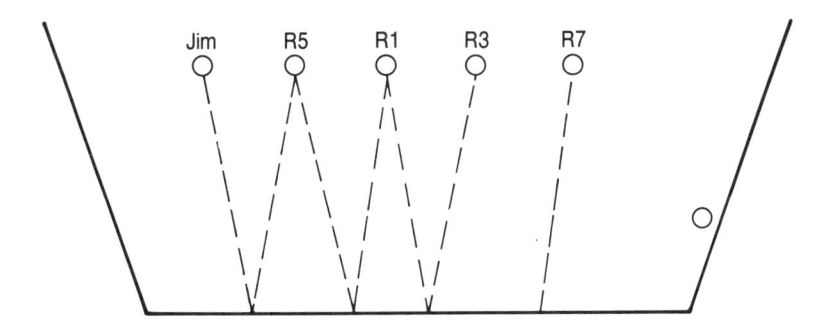

R5: Hi, Nate . . . Pete! What's up!

R1: Men, I've prayed about something for five years now. A project that I know we have all talked about and prayed for.

JIM (*eagerly*): Aucas! You've found 'em Nate!

R1: That's right . . . and only 15 minutes air time from Aranjo.

R5: From my place! If my Indians knew that, there'd be panic.

R1: That's exactly why I called this meeting in secret. If news got out that the Aucas were within striking distance of our Quichuas, a small army would be assembled to go in and clean them out. Something like that would set back missionary efforts another hundred years.

JIM: Maybe some of us should go in to them?

R3: And get murdered like those Shell Oil employees! No, whatever we do, we have to proceed carefully, in God's will. *decisive*

R1: I do have a plan if you want to hear it.

R5: Go ahead, Nate.

R1: We begin by making gift drops over the houses once a week. Using my air-cord release system, we can deliver kettles, machetes, or whatever. We can't even consider going inland to them until they know who we are and that we are friendly.

JIM: But won't that take a lot of time? *(Rises from stool and moves straight DS.)* They don't need pots and pans, they need the Savior!

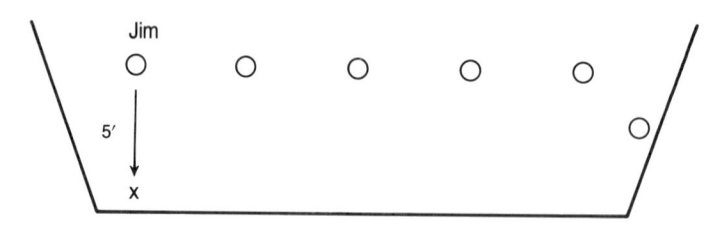

```
          Jim
           O       O       O       O       O
                                                    O
       5' |
           ↓
           X
```

(R3 rises from stool and moves four feet toward audience.)

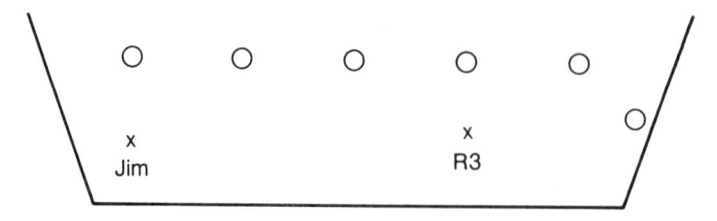

```
           O       O       O       O       O
                                                    O
           X                       X
          Jim                      R3
```

R3: Hey, Jim! We know that, but we have to be careful. On an operation like this, we can't afford to be careless.

JIM: Forgive me if I seem a little overanxious, but this is something that I have held before the throne of grace for over five years.

(R7 rises and moves five feet DS to be in equal stage position with JIM.)

R7: We all have to be careful of being overanxious. We must follow God's timetable.

(R5 *rises and moves four feet DS to be in equal stage position with R3.*)

R5: Something else, Nate. We must remember that it may not be in God's will for all of us to go. Every man must decide for himself.

(R1 *stands directly in front of his stool.*)

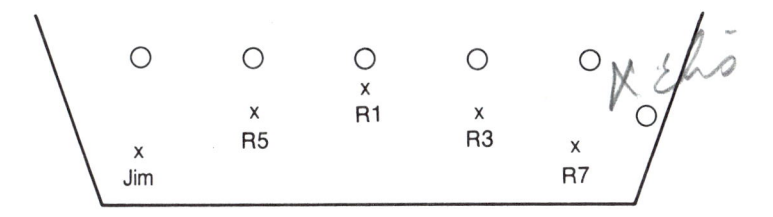

```
   ○      ○      ○      ○      ○
                 x             
   x      x     R1      x      x
  Jim    R5             R3     R7
```

R1: All right, then, two rules: Don't run ahead of God's timetable, and no group pressure. Do we all agree on this basis? (*They nod or smile in agreement. Offstage focus.*)

R1: It's settled. Tomorrow we officially begin "Operation Auca" with the first gift drop. God alone knows where this project will end.

(*If an intermission is desired, the entire cast may leave the stage at this time. If no intermission is desired, the men turn back to their stools and are again seated with their backs to the audience.*)

ACT TWO

ELISABETH: "For a number of years," Nate Saint once wrote, "the Aucas had constituted a hazard to explorers, an embarassment to the Republic of Ecuador, and a challenge to missionaries of the Gospel." Perhaps it would be helpful if I gave a brief history of the Aucas. The name "Auca" is a general term referring to many small groups of Indians that occupy a remote section of western South America. This region was plundered by Spaniards in the 16th century, and the oil companies in the 1950's. Because of this history, all friendly outreaches to the Indians had never succeeded. Some groups of foreigners had given gifts and even received them in return. Feeling that a friendship had been established, protective barriers were let down and murders were always the result. Natives that knew the Aucas well said, "Never, never trust them. They may appear friendly and then they will turn around and kill."

Jim, Pete, Ed, Roger, and Nate left that meeting eager to begin "Operation Auca." Nate had devised a special maneuver for delivering goods to the ground from his plane. By flying in a fairly tight circle and letting out a great length of cord, Nate could cause the end of the cord to be comparatively still near or on the ground, the end of an inverted cone. He could lower a bucket holding a gift or tie something to the cord. The delivery was tricky and painstaking, but the first contact with the Aucas was made through these gift-drops.

41

(*Airplane sketch involves* JIM *and* R1. *They should move their stools DSC close to edge of platform. Stools should be set fairly close together to simulate the crowded effect in the cockpit of a small plane. All flying of plane, lowering of bucket, and sighting of Indians is done in restricted pantomime.*)

JIM: Seems hard to believe that this is already the third flight. I hope that we can at least make visual contact with some Aucas before the month is out.

R1: They'll come in God's time. The gifts are always gone, so they must be taking them.

JIM: There! I see smoke. That big house must be where the head man lives.

R1: See if the kettle is hooked on securely.

JIM: All set.

R1: Let the release go and stand by on the clutch.

JIM: Kettle away. How much cord should I let out?

R1: It depends on visibility . . . about 2,000 feet should do for today.

JIM: I always worry about this thing getting hung up in a tree, . . . how's that!

R1: Looks good, now I'll start to circle and bring it in.

JIM (*Looking through window in amazement at Indians on ground*): Nate! Look . . . Aucas! They're waving at us.

R1: Must be half-dozen of them . . . that one on the end is waving last week's machete at us.

JIM: Then they know the gifts are from us. (JIM *guides* R1's *descent and maneuvering of the bucket.*) A little lower, just a bit . . . some more angle, Nate! . . . easy . . . easy. He's got it! Nate, we've got an Auca on the other end of this thing!

(R1 *and his stool return to original position.* JIM *stays DSC.*)

ELISABETH: The yellow plane flew every week over the primitive strangers bringing them aluminum kettles, buttons, bright ribbons, or anything that would arouse their fancy. Often the Indians would catch the end of the drop line and tie on a gift in return: one week a feathered head band; and the next, a live, tamed parrot. The Indians had responded so much more quickly to these visits than the men had dreamed possible. Each new trip brought the men closer and closer to the realization that they should make the move to fly into the interior and establish a camp near the Auca houses. After searching the surrounding landscape for a possible landing site, Nate decided that the only suitable area was along the Curaray River on a fairly wide sandbar. This target was christened "Palm Beach."

As we sensed the time for the trip to be approaching, an all-out effort was made to obtain bits of the Auca language. A run-away Auca woman named

Dayuma lived on a nearby ranchero. Jim decided to visit her and try to obtain some Auca phrases in the most inconspicuous manner possible.

(*Dayuma Sketch—R6 doubles as Dayuma and comes to sit on* JIM'S *stool. He stands beside her. Offstage focus used.*)

JIM: May I speak with you?

R6: Why?

JIM: I wish to learn of the Aucas.

R6 (*proudly*): Dayuma is Auca.

JIM: I know.

R6: People afraid of Aucas.

JIM: Jim Elliot not afraid.

R6: Only fools not afraid of Aucas!

JIM: My God protects me.

R6: What do you want of me?

JIM: I want to learn some Auca words.

R6: Why . . . what do you want to do with them?

JIM: I . . . I want to write them in my book.

R6: Foolish white missionaries . . . looking at funny black marks in books all time.

JIM: How do you say, "I like you, I want to be your friend"?

R6: Biti, mitit punimupa.

JIM (*he begins to write vigorously in pantomime but doesn't quite make it*): Would you say that again please . . . a little bit slower?

R6: Biti, mitit punimupa . . . Let me see my words in your book. (R6 *reaches straight ahead as does* JIM. *In offstage focus pantomime* R6 *receives and returns* JIM'S *notebook.*) Why put words in book? Words only good when you talk them.

JIM: This makes me to remember how to speak your words. How do you say, "I want to approach you," or, "Let's have a meeting"?

R6: Biti winki pungu amupa.

JIM: How would you ask someone what their name is?

R6: Awum irimi.

JIM: How would you say, "I have some food for you"?

43

(R6 *exits stage area and* JIM *returns to original position.*)

ELISABETH: Thus did Jim learn some key Auca phrases. He was always saying them as he would do mundane tasks around the house. After prayer and Bible reading, the Auca phrases were the last thing to be spoken before Jim went to sleep. The final plans for "Operation Auca" were now in the making.

(*Date-setting sketch. All men come alive and pivot toward audience.*)

JIM: How'd the flight go this week, Nate?

R1: Go ahead, Ed. Tell 'em.

R5: We had circled a couple of times and were coming in for the final turn when right there on the roof of one of the houses we saw the plane!

R3: A plane? What plane?

R1: Those Aucas are a lot sharper than we gave them credit. There was a plane on top of one of the thatched roofs. Must have been carved from some light wood, but it bore a remarkable likeness to my plane.

JIM: They do want us to come!

R7: That does sound like a friendly gesture to me.

R1: It does to me too, and I've done some figuring as far as dates go.

R7: When do we go?

R1: Our target sandbar, "Palm Beach," looks as if it will easily be under water after a good rain so we need to go during the dry season, so that means we go pretty soon. With all of our schedules in mind, I've tried to choose the best time for us to go. The way I figure it, the first flying day in January should be our take-off day.

R7: Sounds good to me!

JIM: Sounds good to all of us. Now, tell us the rest of the plans.

(*All men lower heads out of scene. They stay on stools.*)

ELISABETH: The Christmas season of 1955 was a hard one for all of us. We had little on our hearts and minds except the coming flight to the Aucas. Lurking in each wife's heart was the gnawing fear that this might be the last Christmas with her husband. This season that rings so loudly of home and family is often the hardest for the missionary. The doubts about God's will try to creep in and thoughts turn to friends in the States who live in cozy little split-level homes close to friends and family. In spite of the obviously tremendous need of the field, Jim was continually asked in letters why he left the States to come to such a desolate field. He answered one letter in this way. (*Comes alive, stands.*)

JIM: You wonder why people choose fields far away from the States when young people at home are drifting because no one wants to listen to their problems. I'll tell you why I left. Because those Stateside young people have every opportunity to study, hear, and understand the Word of God in their own language, and these Indians have no opportunity whatsoever. I have had to make a cross of two logs, and lie down on it, to show the Indians what it means to crucify a man. When there is that much ignorance over here and so much knowledge and opportunity over there, I have no question in my mind why God sent me here. Those whimpering Stateside young people will wake up on the Day of Judgment condemned to worse fates than those demon-fearing Indians, because, having a Bible, they were bored with it—while these never heard of such a thing as writing. (*Sits down and lowers head.*)

ELISABETH: On Sunday afternoon, December 10, Nate Saint sat at his typewriter to tell the world why they were going to the Aucas—just in case. In speaking these words, he spoke for them all.

(*All men rise and take positions indicated in diagram. They keep their focus on R1 until it is their turn to speak, then they pivot out and speak toward audience.*)

```
  R1    Jim    R5        R1      R3      R7
  O→    O→     O    ←O    ←O
                    ↓                              O
                    x
```

R1: As we weigh the future and seek the will of God, does it seem right that we should hazard our lives for just a few savages? The Great Commission included every man on earth, and we feel that it is pleasing to God that we should interest ourselves in making an opening into the Auca prison for Christ.

As we have a high old time this Christmas, may we who know Christ hear the cry of the damned as they hurtle headlong into the Christless night without ever a chance. May we be moved with compassion as our Lord was. May we shed tears of repentance for these we have failed to bring out of darkness. Beyond the smiling scenes of Bethlehem may we see the crushing agony of Golgotha. May God give us a new vision of His will concerning the lost and our responsibility.

Would that we could comprehend the lot of these stone-age people who think all men in all the world are killers like themselves. If God would grant us the vision, the word "sacrifice" would disappear from our lips and thoughts!

JIM (*turns out to audience*): We would hate the things that now seem dear to us;

R7 (*turns out to audience*): Our lives would suddenly be too short.

(R5 *and* R3 *turn out to audience and* R5, R3, *and* R1 *speak.*)

R1, R3, R5: We would despise time-robbing distractions and charge the enemy with all our energies in the name of Christ.

ALL: May God help us to judge ourselves by the eternities that separate the Aucas from a comprehension of Christmas and Him, who,

JIM: though He was rich,

R7: yet, for our sakes became poor,

ALL: so that we might, through His poverty, be made rich.

(R2, R4, *and* R6 *come to join men on stage for "Last Night" sketch. This scene is done with traditional onstage focus. Characters strike action poses and then freeze—suggested poses are given in the diagram.* ELISABETH *walks among the freezes as she introduces the wives. At the end of her speech,* ELISABETH *joins the scene, participating with onstage focus.*)

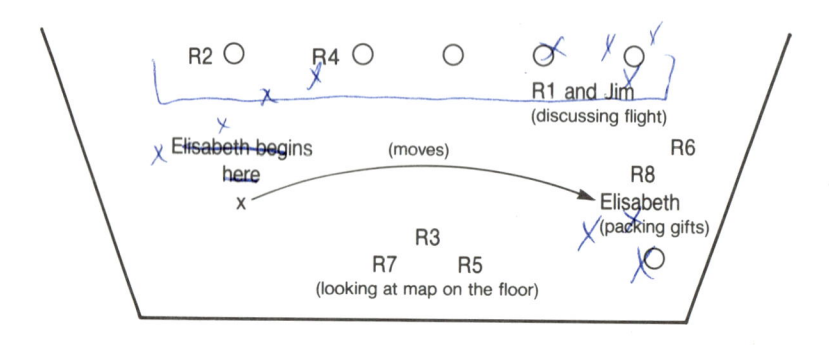

```
        R2 O      R4 O       O        O   O
                                    R1 and Jim
                                   (discussing flight)
    Elisabeth begins      (moves)              R6
         here                                  R8
                                            Elisabeth
                                           (packing gifts)
                             R3
                          R7    R5
                   (looking at map on the floor)
```

(*Last Night sketch*)

ELISABETH: On the night before the operation was to be launched, all the men and their wives met at the Saint's home to discuss final plans and to have one last time of prayer together. (ELISABETH *walks among freezes and points out characters as she names them.*) We were all there—Marj Saint, so wonderfully efficient as the hostess, was busy keeping every plate full of food. Marilou McCully and Barbara Youderian were packing the last of the gift-trinkets. Olive Fleming, still a newlywed, stayed as close to Pete as she could without being obvious, and I was thinking, feeling, praying, and trusting along with the rest. Trying to stay busy with my hands so that my mind would not have time to wander to tomorrow.

(*As soon as* ELISABETH *is in position, freeze ends and scene begins. Onstage focus is used so stage movement should be as in a traditional play.*)

R2: Excuse me (*said to* R3), would you care for a brownie?

R3: No thank you, I've had plenty. We're going to miss your cooking out in the jungle.

R5: That's for sure, excuse me. I need to ask Nate about the portable tree house.

R6: Would you look at this! *(Holds up string of beads in pantomime.)* I'd like to have some of these beads myself. Barbara, some of these Indian women will have nicer jewelry than we do.

R8: We'd better get some more cloth to wrap these mirrors, they break so easily.

ELISABETH: I think this should work. *(Hands R8 more cloth.)* Say, Marj, how about bringing those brownies over here?

R7: *(struggling with words in a humorous way):* Biti-biti . . . pooly-ma-loopi! Jim, I sure don't have the ear for these Auca phrases. Could you give me some more lessons?

R5: I think that we all need the practice. Come over here, Jim, and let's have a school room session. We need to know how to speak to our neighbors when they come calling!

(All men go to far stage right and women to far stage left, leaving DSC empty. R4 moves to this area alone. R3 sees her in offstage focus and comes to stand beside her. They converse with offstage focus.)

(Pete and Olive Sketch)

R3: Olive, what's wrong? Don't you feel well?

R4: I feel like my whole world is shaking on its foundations, just getting ready to fall on me.

R3: Honey, our foundation is in Christ, and He can't come toppling down.

R4: How can they be so light and happy? Don't they realize that tomorrow may be the last time that we ever . . .

R3: Stop that, Olive! You know it isn't good to talk that way.

R4: But Pete! You know it's true.

R3: Maybe it's harder for us because we've had so few months together. But we are in God's will!

R4: Yes, Peter, I know . . . but I just can't understand why God would want us to . . .

R3: We never ask "why," only "when." And tomorrow will provide the "when" for "Operation Auca." If only I could see the flame of life kindled up in the eyes of one Auca, my life would indeed be rich. I know that this is where God wants me, and you must trust me, honey. I love you more than anything on this earth, but God has called me and I must obey . . . I need to obey, and I want to obey.

R4: But Pete! What if those Indians don't want you to come? What if . . . what if you never come back?

R3: Well, if that's the way God wants it to be, I'm ready to die for the salvation of the Aucas.

R4: Oh Pete! If anything ever happened to you, I'd . . .

R3: You'd keep on serving the Lord and He'd keep on sustaining you. Olive, we have to be honest, it would be hard without each other, but God would never fail you. I know that you believe that!

R4: Yes, Pete, I do . . . I just wish I had your strength.

R3: You do, Olive. My strength is in God and God is also in you. Honey, whatever happens, rest assured that it is in God's divine plan.

R4: I know . . . and I understand now but I'm still afraid . . . (*focus changes to onstage and they embrace*) Oh Pete!

(*All characters come to life. Men position themselves in a line just in front of the stools with backs to audience and heads lowered. Women take position suggested in diagram leaving enough room between them for men to come into position when they are to speak.*)

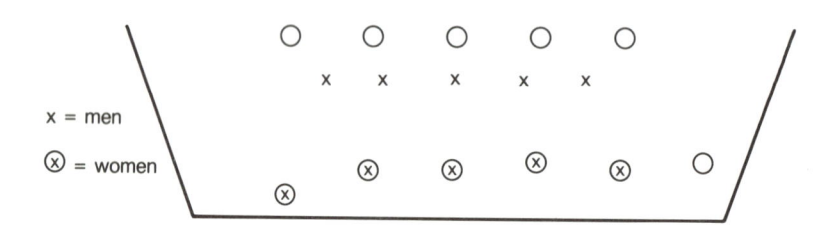

x = men
Ⓧ = women

(*Wives Sketch. Offstage focus used.*)

ELISABETH: Olive?

R4: I'm all right . . . I guess that I just don't have the stamina that the rest of you have.

ELISABETH: We're all afraid, Olive, but God will take care of our boys.

R6: And He'll take care of us too. Didn't you know that this day would come when you married Pete?

R4: Oh sure, we talked about it a lot and back then it even seemed sort of romantic . . . a big adventure . . . but it's not, and tomorrow he'll be gone.

R2: Olive, when Nate asked me to marry him, he told me that I'd always be second to the Lord, and I wouldn't have it any other way. God has given Nate and me more happiness in seven years than most couples have in a lifetime.

R4: But Marj, how can you bear the thought of that happiness ending?

R2: I guess I don't allow the devil to trick me into worrying about it. Keep busy

48

with the work of the Lord and stay close to Him in prayer. Olive, that's the only way you'll be able to come through this thing.

R8: Let's have prayer together before the men get back. It'll just be us and the kids as long as the men are on that sandbar, and praying together will help us stay strong. Not only is God counting on us, but our husbands are too. We can't let them worry about us.

(Wives kneel.)

R4: The Lord is my shepherd.

R2: I shall not want.

ELISABETH: He maketh me to lie down in green pastures.

(Men come alive and turn out to audience, they move to stand by wives.)

R8: He leadeth me beside the still waters.

R6: He restoreth my soul.

ALL WOMEN: He leadeth me in the paths of righteousness for His name's sake.

ALL MEN: Yea though I walk through the valley of the shadow of death, I will fear no evil, for Thou art with me,

ALL WOMEN: Thy rod and thy staff they comfort me.

ALL MEN: Thou preparest a table before me in the presence of mine enemies: Thou anointest my head with oil: my cup runneth over,

ALL CAST: Surely goodness and mercy shall follow me all the days of my life; and I will dwell in the house of the Lord for ever.

(Men kneel by their wives and sing "We Rest on Thee" a capella. This song was sung by the missionaries before they went out to the Aucas. The hymn tune is the same as in "Be Still, My Soul.")

> We rest on Thee, Our Shield and Our Defender!
> We go not forth alone against the foe.
> Strong in Thy strength, safe in Thy keeping tender,
> We rest on Thee, and in Thy name we go.
> Strong in Thy strength, safe in Thy keeping tender,
> We rest on Thee, and in Thy name we go.

(At close of song, men and wives stand slowly. They join hands, with wives standing with their backs to the audience and husbands in front of them facing the audience. They slowly drop hands and husbands turn backs on audience and move to stools. Wives, except ELISABETH, leave the stage area. ELISABETH moves to stand by her stool LSC.)

ELISABETH: The men had spent three days in their little prefabricated tree house when the first Aucas came. Two women and a young man made their way across the river to the missionary camp. Everything possible was done to entertain them: hamburgers were cooked, all types of trinkets were given to them, and the man even got a plane ride with Nate, which delighted him no end. All three of the Aucas seemed friendly and relaxed, and the men praised the Lord for the warmth shown in this first direct contact with these primitive people.

Nate had been spending his nights at Shell Mera and then flying the daily runs between home base and the beach, carrying fresh food, medical supplies, mail, and anything else that was needed. The men had felt from the beginning that no more than five days should be devoted to the project and the fifth day, January 8, dawned bright and clear. As Nate climbed into the plane on that Sunday morning, he called to us:

(R1 *comes alive, pivots out to audience, with offstage focus.*)

R1: So long, girls, pray! I believe that this is the day.

(R1 *lowers head but does not change placement.*)

ELISABETH: According to his custom, Nate flew over the Auca houses on his way to Palm Beach, trying to lead the Indians to the campsight. On this day, however, he was surprised to find the houses almost deserted. In flying along the route to the beach, he sighted a party of about 10 men walking toward the Curaray. The plane had hardly stopped rolling on the beach when Nate, bursting with the news, jumped out and shouted to the men:

(*All men come alive and pivot excitedly out to audience as* R1 *begins to speak.*)

R1: This is it, guys! They're on the way!

R7: How many of them?

R1: Looks like about 10 from up there.

R5: How far away are they?

R3: Let's get some food ready!

R1: They'll be here any minute. Jim, get some wood for the fire. (JIM *steps forward and stoops to get wood and then freezes.*) Rog and Ed get some food ready for them. (R7 *and* R5 *turn to SL and freeze in action poses.*) Pete, hide the guns and ammunition. We don't want them to think us anything but friendly. (R3 *turns USR and freezes.*) I'd better call Marj.

(R1 *sits on center stool. Other men are frozen as he speaks.*)

R1 (*pantomimes holding radio microphone*): Calling Shell Mera . . . Calling Shell Mera . . . Come in, Marj! . . . Honey, I've seen them coming . . . yes! They should be here any minute. Contact the other girls. Pray for us, Marj, this is the day we've waited and prayed for. I'll call again at four-thirty. Good-bye, honey, I love you.

50

(All men come alive, excitedly awaiting arrival of Aucas.)

R7: We've got lunch all ready for them. Maybe the smell of food will hurry them up.

R3: Look! *(Pointing to back of auditorium)* . . . at the edge of the river, they're here!

R5: Don't shout, it might scare them.

JIM: After all these months and years, I can hardly believe it. *(Kneeling, he prays)* Father, thank You for allowing me to bring the gospel to . . .

R1 *(sudden look of horror growing on his face)*: Look! That big fellow is raising his spear!

JIM *(leaping up and gesturing frantically)*: Miti mitit bunimupa!

R5: Stop!

(Each man should make some sound but no real order is necessary. The men are in confusion and this will be evidenced by the looks on their faces and their rapid and defensive gesturing. Each man should strike a pose of defense and pain and then freeze. A complete blackout should be executed at this time. The first four measures of "We Rest on Thee" played at full organ will be very effective now. After the playing of the organ, the men should move into position in front of the stools with backs to audience. Women should also move into position. Check diagram. The wives look directly at ELISABETH *as she speaks for all of them. When all are in position, stage lights come up.)*

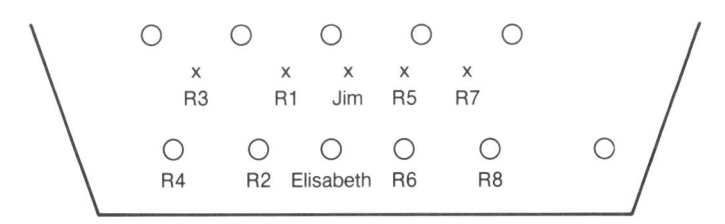

```
    O   O   O   O   O
    x   x   x   x   x
    R3  R1  Jim R5  R7

    O   O   O   O   O
    R4  R2  Elisabeth R6  R8
```

ELISABETH: God supplied our every need and gave us strength that seemed impossible during those first hours of ignorance. When 24 hours had passed without any word from the men, a rescue call went out. The Ecuadorian government sent in troops, private parties of friends went, and mission boards sent in delegations. When the story was finally made known some three days later, we were told that we had all become widows. In her diary, Barbara Youderian recorded the story. She can speak for all of us. *(Turns out to aud.)*

R8: Tonight the captain told us of finding the bodies in the river. God gave me this verse two days ago. Psalm 48:14, "For this God is our God for ever and ever: he will be our guide even unto death." As I came face to face with the news of Rog's death, my heart was filled with praise. He was worthy of his home going. Help me, Lord, to be both mommy and daddy. I've explained to Beth that Daddy is now in heaven living with Jesus, but she can't under-

51

stand why he won't come down and play with her once in a while. I wrote a letter to the mission family, trying to explain the peace I have. I want to be free of self-pity. It is a tool of Satan to rot away a life. I am sure that this is the perfect will of God. The Lord has closed our hearts to grief and hysteria, and filled in with His perfect peace.

(R8 *returns to her position and* ELISABETH *takes CS.*)

ELISABETH: The other widows and I have received countless messages from all over the world, telling of young men and women who have made decisions for Christ because of what happened to our husbands. God's perfect plan was fulfilled and His name glorified. After the men's death, Nate's sister, Rachel, and I kept working to reach the Aucas, the other wives went back to their various tribes and stations where they had served with their husbands, another pilot continued to make gift drops to the Indians, and the seed gradually bore fruit.

(*Men come alive and turn to look at* ELISABETH.)

Today there is a strong church among the Aucas and some of the men who killed our husbands are now preaching the saving grace of Christ, looking forward to the day when they can thank our husbands in glory. It is our prayer tonight, that the same God who ruled the hearts and lives of these five missionaries is also ruling your heart. Let God have His way with you.

(*Men step forward and stand by wives facing the audience. Last line of play is said in unison by cast.*)

ALL: He is no fool who gives what he cannot keep, to gain what he cannot lose.

(*Cast leaves stage at this time. A call for dedication or salvation may be extended to the audience.*)

Glossary

Apron .... The area of the stage closest to the audience; usually runs width of stage.

Come alive .... The moment a performer becomes animated and an active participant in a scene.

Drop out of scene......... The moment when an active character in a scene becomes inactive. This allows the character to "leave the stage" as far as the audience is concerned. This is accomplished by turning the back to audience or lowering the head.

Freeze .... The cessation of all bodily movement to create a special stage effect; best accomplished when characters are in strong action poses.

Pantomime .... The execution of some manual task without the presence of the physical property (prop) in question.

Prop .... Any physical property such as a sword, stool, book, or any piece of equipment.

Turn into scene .... When a character who has been "out of a scene" comes alive, and turns around or raises his head to become part of the scene.

Wings .... The offstage area on either side of the playing area.

STAGE DIAGRAM

USR	USC	USL
upstage right	upstage center	upstage left
CSR	CS	CSL
center stage right	center stage	center stage left
DSR	DSC	DSL
downstage right	downstage center	downstage left